PICTURE HISTORY
OF THE
SS *United States*

William H. Miller, Jr.

DOVER PUBLICATIONS, INC.
Mineola, New York

For Tom Chirby
Who so deeply appreciates classical liners
like the SS *United States*

Bibliographical Note

Picture History of the SS United States is a new work, first pub-
lished by Dover Publications, Inc., in 2003.

Library of Congress Cataloging-in-Publication Data

Miller, William H., 1948–
    Picture history of the SS United States / William H. Miller, Jr.
        p. cm.
    Includes bibliographical references.
    ISBN 0-486-42839-7 (pbk.)
    1. United States (Steamship)—History—Pictorial works.
I. Title.

VM383.U5M53 2003
387.2'432'0973—dc21

                                                                2003043463

Book design by Carol Belanger Grafton

Manufactured in the United States of America
Dover Publications, Inc., 31 East 2nd Street, Mineola, N.Y. 11501

Foreword

The SS *United States* began her record-breaking maiden voyage on July 3, 1952—my fourth birthday. I like to think that my relationship with America's maritime champion began that day. As a boy, I built models of the *United States*, but it wasn't until years later, in the early 1960s, that I first laid eyes on her. My mother and I were driving on Manhattan's Henry Hudson Parkway, then down the West Side Highway. In the distance, I could see the huge red, white, and blue stacks, and as we approached the pier, I said to my mother, "Slow down, slow down!" As we passed the great ship, her paintwork gleaming in the summer sun, I exclaimed, "I want that!" My mother said, "You can't have her, dear. She belongs to someone else." I didn't care. It was love at first sight.

More years passed. I knew the *United States* had been taken out of service and laid-up, but never thought that she would come back into my life. In 1984, her then-owner, Richard Hadley, decided to auction off her contents. Everything was to go: furniture, china, glassware, silver, works of art, linens, navigation instruments, clocks, kitchen equipment—practically anything that could be removed from the ship. By then, I had moved to New York and decided to go to the auction.

The auction took place in Norfolk, Virginia, right next to one of the docks where the *United States* had been sitting idle for nearly fifteen years. Those years had not been kind to the ship, but from a distance she still looked every inch the thoroughbred racer that William Francis Gibbs designed her to be. I, along with thousands of others, was able to tour the ship. I marveled at her size and explored all the public rooms, cabins, and working spaces, and even met her last captain, Commodore Leroy Alexanderson.

As the auction began, the prices for even the smallest lots were breathtaking. But as the week went on, prices began to drop . . . and I began to buy. When finished, I had the beginning of what has become a personal collection of ocean liner furnishings and decorative arts. So, in a small way, I proved my mother wrong. I did end up with at least a part of the finest ship America has ever produced.

But what is there about the *United States* that continues to fascinate? Is it her size, her speed, and beautiful lines, or the 1950s glamour that she represents? It is all these things, and perhaps a yearning for a simpler, possibly more elegant, time. Whatever the future may bring for America's greatest liner, for fifty years, she has captured the imagination of her builders, her passengers and crew, of maritime writers and historians, and of star-struck fans like me. The voyage that Bill Miller will take you on in the following pages celebrates those fifty years, and is a fitting tribute to a true American champion.

CHARLES W. HOWLAND
New York City
March 2002

Charles Howland owns a major collection of ocean liner memorabilia, highlighted by many pieces from the SS *United States*.

Acknowledgements

Much like the crew aboard the *United States* herself, many hands were needed to produce this work. Photographs must be collected, borrowed mostly from kind, generous, and very patient friends and fellow ship enthusiasts, and then organized by chapters. Interviews had to be done and certain facts needed to be checked. Consequently, a good-sized "crew" emerged. All of them are in some way fascinated by this great ship, her accomplishments, her place in ocean liner history and, of course, as a centerpiece of national pride.

Of course, I plan to continue to collect more and more photos—those unusual, unpublished views of passenger ships large and small—and to amass more interviews—those insights that add to the story and our understanding of these ships. I am especially indebted to the publishers who continue to produce books on ocean liners, and certainly Dover Publications is on the very top of my list. For almost twenty-five years, beginning with that first morning meeting and introduction in their Lower Manhattan offices on Varick Street, I have cherished our relationship. Dover is a superb producer of books. Until that time, they had never done a book on passenger ships before, and today we can count over a dozen titles together. I have done historic overviews, as well as works on various countries and shipowners of their fleets, but this is my first with Dover on a particular ship. Indeed, I was delighted when they accepted the project on the *United States* just as she had reached her fiftieth year. I am especially grateful to the late Hayward Cirker, the founder of Dover, for always being such a great inspiration and for personally fostering some titles. Great thanks also to Clarence Strowbridge for taking on new projects, and to Jenny Bak for her superb editorial assistance. Jenny has refined the original text, improved it and, with her highly trained eye, found inconsistencies, omissions, those little errors. She has weeded out all the mistakes and brought this title to a higher level.

Very special thanks to a team of fine friends and generous contributors headed by Richard Faber, the New York-based memorabilia collector and dealer. He offers resources that are unmatchable. A grand nod of thanks to my business partner, Abe Michaelson, who, in over fifteen years, has packed and sent books to the far corners of the earth. Kindest appreciation to Charles Howland for his fine, reflective foreword. I would like to make special note of several other invaluable assistants: Ernest Arroyo, Frank Braynard, Tom Cassidy, Norman Knebel, Captain Ed Squire, and Dan Trachtenberg. They are joined with a first-class team of still other supportive friends: Commodore & Mrs. Leroy Alexanderson, Robert Allan, Michael Cassar, Tom Chirby, Anthony Cooke, the late Frank Cronican, Frank Duffy, Laurence Dunn, Linda Fastbach, John Ferguson, the late John Gillespie, Nico Guns, Brad Hatry, Andy Hernandez, Ray Kane, Dimitri Kaparis, Arnold Kludas, Peter Knego, Jan Loeff, Victor Marinelli, Mitchell Mart, Richard K. Morse, William Muller, Peter Newall, Hisashi Noma, Robert Pelletier, Frank Pichardo, Mario Pulice, Rich Romano, Robert Russell, Sal Scannella, Der Scutt, Michael Shernoff, Don Stoltenberg, the late Everett Viez, and Alan Zamchick. Other fine contributors include Dietmar Borchert, Philippe Brebant, Tom Cangialosi, Stephen Card, Luis Miguel Correia, Harley & Barbara Crossley, Martin Cox, Andrew Dibben, Michael Dollenbacher, Alex Duncan, Maurizio Eliseo, James Flood, John Geary, Hans Hoffmann, David Hutchings, Andy Kilk, Joe Kowalski, Peter Lancaric, Robert Lloyd, Paolo Piccione, David Powers, Fred Rodriguez, Robert Russell, Selim San, Antonio Scrimali, Stephen L. Tacey, Gordon Turner, Steffen Weirauch, Al Wilhelmi, David Williams, Martin Wismer, and Victor H. Young. Companies, other organizations, and even websites that have helped include American Classic Voyages, American President Lines, Chandris Lines, Crystal Cruises, Flying Camera, Inc., Grace Line, Maritime Matters, Matson Line, Moore-McCormack Lines, Moran Towing & Transportation Company, Newport News Shipbuilding & Dry Dock Company, Port Authority of New York & New Jersey, the *Queen Mary* Museum, Steamship Historical Society of America (especially the Long Island chapter), United States Lines, United States Merchant Marine Museum Collection, and the World Ship Society (especially the Port of New York Branch).

Introduction

There were no celebrations on July 3, 2002, at least in New York, but it was a rather special date in maritime history, especially that of America. Exactly fifty years before, the super liner *United States* left her berth at the foot of West 46th Street and began her remarkable maiden voyage westward. She made the crossing to England in the swiftest time yet—3 days, 10 hours, and 40 minutes—and captured the prized Blue Riband of the Atlantic, taking the honor from Britain's *Queen Mary*. Triumphantly, the *United States* brought honor to her nation, her owners, and those who designed and built her. Instantly, she became the most famous, most publicized, and most popular passenger ship afloat. "There was nothing quite like her in the 1950s," remembered a British friend, himself a master of merchant vessels. "She was the floating pride of America. Alone, she symbolized the brilliant technology of, what was then, the most advanced nation on earth."

This book has been created to help celebrate the very being of the *United States*. Although she sailed commercially for only seventeen years, she is well remembered to this day. I am continually asked about her current status. Can she be converted to a contemporary cruise ship? Will she sail again? Or will she become a stationary hotel, convention center, or museum? On the busy ocean-liner collectibles market, she is of top interest and one of the highest sellers, ranking with the likes of the ill-fated *Titanic* and the ultra-extravagant *Normandie*. A cocktail glass, a mounted ashtray, and even a slightly shabby stateroom footstool fetch hefty prices.

The *United States* was innovative, successful—a grand flag-waver. Steamship historian Frank Braynard once dubbed her "a star-spangled giant." She was, of course, created for a different era, with different needs and different concerns. She was very much an outgrowth of the Second World War, when Washington eyed big liners as useful troopships to call forth should another military emergency develop. To some in the late 1940s and early '50s, World War III was not unthinkable. The *United States* was specially designed for easy conversion from 2,000 peacetime passengers to as many as 15,000 troops within days. The Pentagon was most enthused. But America also wanted a serious contender on the still-lucrative commercial transatlantic passenger run to and from Europe. The new national flagship had to surpass all those from Europe, namely the British with their celebrated pair *Queen Mary* and *Queen Elizabeth*. "American liners had been in the shadows, in second place, for far too long," observed Braynard, who authored a book on the *United States* in 1979.

Throughout the 1950s, she superbly fulfilled that commercial role. Fortunately, she was never called to war duty. But the '60s ushered in lasting changes. Jet airplanes gave the airlines an even greater hold on trans-ocean travel, and big liners like the *United States* lost their clientele, even among the most loyal. She lost money, and then even more money. By 1968–69, she was operating deeply in the red. Furthermore, the government, which had paid most of her construction costs and then provided operating subsidies, had lost interest. There would be, they predicted, little if any need for such a troopship in the foreseeable future.

In November 1969, the wondrous, still pristine *United States* began her long sleep: lay-up, silence and darkness, stripping down, deterioration . . . then deepening, almost irretrievable decay. Through it all, her uncertain future has been spiced by continuous rumors: the schemes, the plans, the gossip. In fact, she has now been idle longer than any other major liner in history. As I write this, she lies dormant at a Philadelphia pier—a cold, rust-streaked, largely barren ship. She is a symbol of forgotten technology, a representative of a different kind of transport, a faded heiress of a bygone era. But, on April 14, 2003, there came splendid—if surprising—news: Miami-based Norwegian Cruise Lines announced that they planned to buy, refit, and modernize the 51-year-old super liner, turning her into a contemporary cruise ship that would sail under the U.S. flag. A "second" maiden voyage would come after all.

On the occasion of the fiftieth anniversary of her momentous inaugural as well as her early success and her place overall in ocean liner history, we owe it to her to take another look at the greatest American ocean liner of all time—the brilliant SS *United States*. Now, the lines are being cast as we head on a sentimental voyage.

BILL MILLER
Secaucus, New Jersey
Spring 2003

Picture Credits

American President Lines: page 45 (top and bottom)

Author's Collection: page 6

Frank O. Braynard Collection: pages 3, 4 (top), 41 (top and bottom), 48 (top)

Cronican-Arroyo Collection: pages 4 (bottom), 5, 10 (top), 12, 17, 33 (top), 34 (bottom), 36–37, 44, 61 (top), 63 (bottom), 66 (top), 72–73, 75 (top and bottom), 84 (top and bottom), 86, 94 (top), 95 (top and bottom), 96 (top and bottom), 98, 101 (bottom), 102 (all), 103 (top and bottom)

Frank Duffy Collection: pages 30, 109

Alex Duncan: pages 8 (bottom), 10 (bottom), 16 (top), 19 (bottom), 22 (top), 23, 28

Richard Faber Collection: page 77 (all)

Flying Camera, Inc.: pages 46, 47 (bottom), 51, 74, 92

John Gillespie Collection: page 24

Gillespie-Faber Collection: pages 33 (bottom), 35, 38 (top), 40, 42 (top), 49 (bottom), 50 (top), 93 (top)

Grace Line: pages 34 (top), 42 (bottom)

Peter Knego: pages 20 (top), 52, 111 (top and bottom), 112, 113 (all), 114 (top and bottom)

Matson Line: pages 48 (bottom), 49 (top)

Moore-McCormack Lines: page 32

Moran Towing & Transportation Company: page 38 (bottom)

Richard K. Morse Collection: page 18

Newport News Shipbuilding & Dry Dock Company: pages 64 (bottom), 65, 67, 68–69

Norfolk Shipbuilding & Dry Dock Company: page 110

Paolo Piccione Collection: page 47 (top)

Port Authority of New York and New Jersey: pages 70 (bottom), 78–79, 80, 82 (bottom)

Fred Rodriguez Collection: page 19 (top)

Antonio Scrimali: page 39

Stephen L. Tacey: page 20 (bottom)

United States Lines: page 7 (top and bottom), 8 (top), 9, 13, 14 (bottom), 15, 16 (bottom), 26-27, 29, 54 (bottom), 55, 56 (top and bottom), 57, 58 (top and bottom), 59, 60, 62, 63 (top), 64 (top), 71 (bottom), 76, 81 (top and bottom), 82 (top), 83, 85, 88, 89 (bottom), 90 (top and bottom), 91 (top and bottom), 94 (bottom), 97 (bottom), 104, (top and bottom), 105 (top and bottom)

United States Merchant Marine Academy: pages 70 (top), 100 (bottom), 101 (top), 106 (bottom)

United States Merchant Marine Museum: pages 22 (bottom), 25, 50 (bottom), 54 (top), 61 (bottom), 66 (bottom), 71 (top), 89 (top), 93 (bottom), 97 (top), 99 (top and bottom), 100 (top), 106 (top), 107

Everett Viez Collection: page 14 (top)

Martin Wismer: page 115

V. H. Young and L. A. Sawyer: page 43

Contents

⌒

CHAPTER I

United States Lines: The Early Fleet

By the end of the First World War, the world's collective passenger fleet was devastated. Britain's Cunard Line lost more than half of its ships alone. Others, like the White Star Line, lost their leading ships, while the once prominent Germans, namely the Hamburg America Line and North German Lloyd, were crippled. Their losses were high, and almost all remaining passenger ships were taken by the Allied nations as reparations. In fact, the three largest liners then afloat, Hamburg America's *Imperator*, *Vaterland*, and the incomplete *Bismarck*, changed flags. They became the British *Berengaria*, the American *Leviathan*, and the British *Majestic*, respectively. Many other ex-German liners were in American hands, some still serving as troop transports and others waiting at anchor for calls to commercial services following Yankee makeovers. Even a trio of grand four-stackers, once the pride of the Kaiser's transatlantic fleet, were kept in mothballs, rumored to be awaiting a revival as rebuilt, modernized luxury ships under the Stars and Stripes.

The U.S. government saw this great gap in North Atlantic passenger service by 1920, and was also pressed to use the surplus of ex-German tonnage on its hands. Washington also wanted to strengthen the national merchant marine, a result of the eye-opening shortage of ships of all types during World War I, and to accommodate a potential need for troopships in the future. And so, the United States Mail Steamship Company was formed in 1920 to operate those government-owned passenger ships as commercial ventures. The new firm opened for business in the summer of 1920, and the first trip came that August, when the 9,900-ton *Susquehanna*, originally North German Lloyd's *Rhein* of 1899, set sail from Hoboken for Bremen, and then onward to Danzig. Westbound immigration was still very much inherent in the thinking, and was reflected in her re-configured capacity for 500 passengers in cabin-class, and as many as 2,500 in third-class.

Expansion was rapid—far too rapid, in fact. Within a month, the seventy-eight-passenger, single-class *Panhandle State* and her five sisters began a New York–London service. In January, the *Princess Matoika*, formerly the German *Prinzess Alice*, inaugurated a western Mediterranean service to Naples and Genoa. The more pressing and prestigious North Atlantic route had preference, however, and soon other liners were assigned to that trade: the *Hudson*, once the German *Hamburg*; the *Potomac*, the former *Neckar*, also ex-German; and two large liners, the 23,788-ton *George Washington* and her slightly smaller sister, the 22,622-ton *America*. These were two of the largest and most popular in the German fleet prior to the war. Within eight months, the brand-new United States Mail Steamship Company was operating no less than ten passenger ships.

Unfortunately, the new company was incurring massive losses, lacked adequate operating capital, and suffered from inexperienced management. By the summer of 1921, the U.S. government, namely the U.S. Shipping Board, stepped in and took over all aspects of United States Mail. Quick reorganization followed and, in August, the company was given new management and improved finances, and was renamed United States Lines, a name that would be in use for the next sixty-five years. Soon afterward, two large combination passenger-cargo liners joined the fleet—the *Peninsula State* and the *Lone Star State*, which were briefly renamed the *President Pierce* and *President Taft*, respectively, before being permanently renamed the *President Roosevelt* and *President Harding*. That naming theme proved popular, and soon the *Centennial State* and her five sisters were given presidential names as well. Even some older ships changed, such as the *Princess Matoika* to the *President Arthur*, and the *Hudson* to the *President Fillmore*. Others were, of course, very popular as they were, such as the *America* and the *George Washington*. In 1923, in something of a giant step, the company added the rebuilt, Americanized, 59,956-ton *Leviathan*, the former German *Vaterland*. She was one of the largest ships of any kind then afloat, and, for the first time in memory, placed the United States in the major leagues of Atlantic passenger shipping. She was easily one of the eight greatest liners of her day, with the others being the *Berengaria*, *Aquitania*, and *Mauretania* of Cunard; the *Majestic*, *Olympic*, and *Homeric* of White Star; and the *France* of the French Line. Soon, the reviving Germans would add their first major liner since the war, North German Lloyd's *Columbus*. The *Leviathan* was prominent in this select group of so-called "floating palaces," popular to an extent, but never very profitable, quite sadly.

Overall, United States Lines prospered and made significant, cost-cutting changes. The five passenger ships used on the New York-London service were replaced by more practical, twelve-berth freighters run by a new subsidiary, the American Merchant Line. A third medium-sized liner, the 17,900-ton *Republic*, formerly Hamburg America's *President Grant* left over from World War I, joined the *America* and the *George Washington*. Unfortunately, the far larger *Leviathan* was left without a similar-sized running mate.

By the late 1920s, United States Lines had grown and reached well beyond the North Atlantic liner trade. The company owned the Panama Pacific Line, which ran three deluxe passenger ships, the 20,000-ton sisters *California*, *Pennsylvania*, and *Virginia*, on an intercoastal run between New York, the Panama Canal, Los Angeles, and San Francisco. As well as being the first commercial ships to use turbo-electric drive, they offered very high standard passenger accommodations, which were often said to be equal to those on the Atlantic liners. Another subsidiary was the American Pioneer Line, which operated no less than twenty-one diesel-driven freighters from the U.S. East Coast to Pacific ports, to the Far East, South Pacific islands, Australia, and New Zealand. United States Lines also owned several other freighter firms, including the American France Line, the Oriole Line, and the American Hampton Roads Line.

There were hard times in the late twenties, however. Money problems worsened, primarily complicated by extremely costly American sea-going labor and Prohibition laws, which kept all U.S.-flag ships dry. It became increasingly difficult to compete with the likes of the *Berengaria*, the *Majestic*, or the brand-new *Ile de France*. The government had little choice but to sell off United States Lines in March 1929 to a private buyer, P. W. Chapman & Company. The price was $16 million for eleven ships. The sale contract included, among other items, federal assistance toward two 45,000-ton super liners that could run with the fleetmate-short, money-losing *Leviathan*. But further troubles were ahead—in fact, within six months. Soon after the Wall Street crash that October, transatlantic travel began its downward spiral. The million voyagers of 1930 had slumped to half that within five years.

The new owners made some quick changes. The aging *George Washington*, *America*, and *Republic* were dropped. Plans for new tonnage were altered from two 45,000-tonners to a more practical pair of 24,000-ton liners, the *Manhattan* and *Washington* of 1932–33. Two more American Merchant Line combo ships were added to reinforce the passenger and freight trades to England, while the giant *Leviathan* spent more and more time in lay-up, especially in the winter off-season. But then the Chapman Company itself collapsed in October 1931, overwhelmed by the Depression, with coffers that were all but dry. Once again, the federal government entered the picture, foreclosed on mortgages, and resold the entire operation to a newly organized holding company, United States Lines Company of Nevada, itself an arm of the International Mercantile Marine, once a huge and powerful shipping combine. Again, new management took hold and costs were trimmed. Any thoughts for a big new liner to replace the *Leviathan* were soon dropped, and, as that rust-streaked, faded ship sailed off to the breakers in the winter of 1938, a third new liner was ordered—smaller and more practical. Slightly larger than the *Manhattan* and *Washington*, the 33,900-ton *America* was due in the summer of 1940 for Atlantic crossings to Europe. Indeed, further change, disruption, and uncertainty were ahead.

⤳ LEVIATHAN

The 59,956-ton *Leviathan* is the largest passenger liner ever to sail under the U.S. flag. She had been the largest ship of any kind then afloat when completed in May 1914 as Hamburg America Line's *Vaterland*. Routed between Hamburg, the Channel ports, and New York, she was, in a great miscalculation, left at her Hoboken pier when the Germans started World War I three months later, in August. Left idle for nearly three years, she was seized by the Americans after the U.S. entry into the war in the spring of 1917. That July, she began sailing as a high-capacity troopship, the *Leviathan*, until October 1919. The great ship is seen here (*above*) arriving at Hoboken in 1918 with no less than six tugs in attendance along her starboard side. [Built by Blohm & Voss Shipbuilders, Hamburg, Germany, 1914. 54,282 gross tons; 950 feet long; 101 feet wide; 35-foot draft. Steam turbines, quadruple screw. Service speed 23 knots. 3,391 passengers (970 first-class, 542 second-class, 944 third-class, 935 fourth-class).]

The fate and use of the giant *Leviathan* was uncertain for some time and so she sat idle, neglected, and rusting at her Hoboken berth. She was finally transferred to United States Lines in 1922 and sent down to the Newport News Shipyard for a complete restoration. A young architect named William Francis Gibbs supervised the massive task, which was further complicated when the bitter Germans refused to hand over proper plans and blueprints of the ship. Consequently, Gibbs had to virtually redesign the existing vessel. He later designed Matson Line's *Malolo*, considered to be one of the most advanced and safest liners afloat. The *Leviathan* is outbound in this view from October 1927 *(opposite,*

top), having just sailed from New York's Pier 86, while the *Malolo*, inbound on her maiden voyage, moves into the same berth.

The *Leviathan* was every bit one of the "floating palaces" of the 1920s North Atlantic. Her magnificent First-Class Social Hall, dominated by a glass skylight-ceiling, is seen here *(above)*.

Celebrities such as Tom Mix, Gloria Swanson, and Queen Marie of Rumania sailed aboard the great *Leviathan*. Here we see the verandah sitting area of one of the ship's grand Verandah Suites *(opposite, bottom)*. In the 1920s, it was priced from $300 per person, per day, for the six-day trips to and from Southampton and Cherbourg.

The *Leviathan* ran single-handedly: she did not have a proper running mate or even an equivalent companion ship within United States Lines, and therefore her schedules were unbalanced. Meanwhile, Cunard and White Star ran three big liners on the North Atlantic run and so provided a weekly departure in each direction. United States Lines was at a disadvantage with their otherwise famous superliner. Consequently, the *Leviathan* lost many potential passengers and, coupled with extremely high operational costs, lost more money. By 1930, she was already known to be one of the least successful liners on the Atlantic. Thereafter, she was often laid-up and, in 1934, made only four round-trip crossings. Laid-up permanently after that, she spent some time at dock in Manhattan before being moved to a berth across the Hudson, at the foot of Second Street in Hoboken. She is seen here *(above)*, in a view dated August 11, 1935, with six liners at the Chelsea Piers. From top to bottom are the *Manhattan*, United States Lines; *Georgic* and *Majestic*, both Cunard-White Star; *Leviathan*; *Pennland*, Red Star Line; and the *Paris*, French Line.

∿ GEORGE WASHINGTON
Having been built for North German Lloyd, the *George Washington* was, like many German liners of that era, given an American name to lure more third-class immigrant passengers on westbound sailings. Many Europeans felt that a ship with an American or American-sounding name would help with their processing and admittance on Ellis Island. Like the *Vaterland* (later *Leviathan*), the *George Washington* was left at her Hoboken berth when World War I began in the summer of 1914. She was seized by the U.S. government in the spring of 1917 and refitted as the Allied USS *George Washington*. Popular with the troops, she was

soon fondly dubbed "Big George." Seen here during a subsequent refit in the big graving dock at the Boston Naval Shipyard *(opposite, top)*, she was refitted for passenger service in 1921 and sailed for United States Lines for over ten years, until laid-up in 1932. While she might have been scrapped, the Second World War saw the 32-year-old ship reactivated in 1941 as the USS *Catlin* for the Navy Department. She was briefly loaned to the British, but her aged machinery made her troublesome, and so she was returned promptly. Following repairs, she resumed service with the Navy until damaged by a fire at New York in March 1947. Unrepaired, she was moved to Baltimore and laid-up, where a second fire destroyed much of the ship on January 17, 1951. Her final remains were broken-up that August. [Built by Vulkan Shipyards, Stettin, Germany, 1909. 25,570 gross tons; 723 feet long; 72 feet wide. Steam quadruple-expansion engines, twin screw. Service speed 18½ knots. 2,500 passengers in 1921 (573 first-class, 442 second-class, 1,485 third-class).]

∿ PRESIDENT ROOSEVELT
United States Lines ran a number of large passenger-cargo ships, members of the so-called 502 and 535 classes. The largest and best known of these were the sisters *President Roosevelt*, seen here leaving her Chelsea berth *(opposite, bottom)*, and *President Harding*. They offered longer, more leisurely voyages between New York and Northern Europe: seven days to Cobh, eight to Plymouth and Le Havre, and ten all the way to Hamburg. Fares ranged from $129 in first-class to $82 in third-class in the mid-1930s. [Built by New York Shipbuilding Corporation, Camden, New Jersey, 1922. 13,869 gross tons; 535 feet long; 65 feet wide. Steam turbines, twin screw. Service speed 17 knots. 437 passengers (201 cabin-class, 236 third-class).]

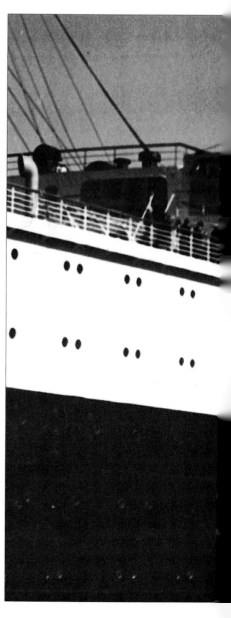

The Cabin-Class Dining Room aboard the *President Roosevelt* had a pleasant, inviting, and unpretentious quality about it (*opposite, top*). Note the arc-shaped glass ceiling. Later, the *Roosevelt* served as a troopship during the war before being scrapped in 1948. The *Harding* was sold to the Belgians and renamed *Ville de Bruges* in February 1940, but was bombed and sunk by the Germans four months later.

∾ AMERICAN TRADER

For the New York–London service of their subsidiary, American Merchant Line, United States Lines used as many as seven converted transports, later refitted as twelve-passenger freighters, but modified still later to carry from 74 to 120 one-class passengers. There was the *American Merchant, American Shipper, American Banker, American Farmer, American Trader (opposite, bottom), American Importer,* and *American Traveler.* Sold to the still-neutral Belgians in early 1940, all but the *American Banker* was lost. With greatly expanded low-fare quarters, she went on to sail as the passenger-carrying *City of Athens, Protea,* and finally *Arosa Kulm* before being scrapped in 1959. [Built by American Shipbuilding Corporation, Hog Island, Pennsylvania, 1920. 7,430 gross tons; 448 feet long; 58 feet wide. Steam turbines, single screw. Service speed 15 knots. 74 one-class passengers.]

∾ WASHINGTON and MANHATTAN

While twin 45,000-ton luxury liners were at first planned for the early 1930s, United States Lines scaled down their plans, especially in view of the Depression, to two more conservative 24,000-ton sister ships. The *Manhattan* was commissioned in August 1932, and the *Washington,* seen here departing from Pier 61 at New York in 1939 (*below*), in May 1933. Part of a transatlantic group of medium-sized passenger ships known as "cabin liners," their cabin-class quarters dominated their three classes, and eliminated first-class altogether. This was an effort to offer lower fares in the lean Depression years.

The two liners also ran occasional cruises such as five days to Bermuda for $55 and two weeks to the Caribbean for $120. While sailing in the new, luxurious age with the likes of the French *Normandie* (1935) and Britain's *Queen Mary* (1936), the *Manhattan* and *Washington* were very popular, successful ships. They were inspirations for a third, larger version—the *America* of 1940. [Built by New York Shipbuilding Corporation, Camden, New Jersey, 1933. 24,289 gross tons; 705 feet long; 86 feet wide. Steam turbines, twin screw. Service speed 20 knots. 1,239 passengers (582 cabin-class, 461 tourist-class, 196 third-class).]

Intermingled with some examples of contemporary, 1930s style decor, the *Washington* and the *Manhattan* had some period and theme-style public areas. Here we see the Cabin-Class Smoking Room aboard the *Manhattan (above)*, a space decorated in an American Indian theme.

Beginning in the fall of 1939, the *Manhattan* and the *Washington*, along with other company ships and chartered passenger vessels, made urgent sailings out of European ports (Bordeaux, Lisbon, Marseilles, Genoa, and Naples among them) to bring American tourists, workers and their families, government personnel, and even refugees away from increasingly troubled Europe. The war had started for the British and the Germans, but American ships were still neutral and supposedly not vulnerable to attack. U.S.-flag vessels actually wore huge neutrality markings along their sides and this special effect included top-deck aerial markings, as well as illuminated signs for nighttime sailings. The *Manhattan* and *Washington* were later turned over to the U.S. Navy, becoming the high-capacity troopships *Wakefield* and *Mount Vernon*, respectively. The *Wakefield* caught fire off Halifax on September 3, 1942 and was badly damaged, but subsequently repaired. She was mothballed in May 1946, never to sail again, and was broken-up for scrap in the summer of 1964. The *Mount Vernon* was returned to United States Lines in 1947 and restored, but as a low-fare, all-austerity-class Atlantic liner, assisting the *America* on the run to Southampton, Le Havre, and Bremerhaven. She is seen here in 1948 *(below)*, her wartime radar mast still in place above the wheelhouse. She was transferred, in late 1951, to MSTS (Military Sea Transportation Service) for "government only" service before being mothballed as well, in February 1953. She went to New Jersey shipbreakers in the summer of 1965.

CHAPTER II

❧

The *America:* A Grand Forerunner

Turmoil in Europe began on September 1, 1939, when ferocious Nazi bombs slammed into Poland. The day before, at Newport News in Virginia, the sparkling new *America* was launched in a cheerful, high-spirited event that included a naming and christening ceremony by Mrs. Eleanor Roosevelt, the wife of the American president. As the *America* slipped into the James River, her proud owners and builders cheered—she was the new flagship of the American merchant marine, one of the most advanced ships afloat and, most importantly, the start of a massive shipbuilding program in the United States. She was the start of a great "build-up of the fleet." Thirteen years and some 6,000 ships later, by 1952, her successor, the brilliant *United States*, was the last in this particular program.

By the time she was completed in the summer of 1940, and when her intended European service was canceled, the *America* was already being appraised as the most beautiful ship in the American fleet. She was modern looking, very trim, and had the idyllic balance of two masts with two evenly slanted, winged funnels. Designed by the outstanding William Francis Gibbs, she was, in fact, based on one of his earlier projects, the four sisters of the *Santa Rosa* class of 1932–33 for the Grace Line. They were, in many ways, the predecessors to the *America*, a point especially evident by their rather similar twin-funnel design. The new *America* was also fast, advanced, and

said to be the safest merchant ship then afloat. While not a record-breaker, this new liner came in an age—the late 1930s—that produced such similar-sized liners as the Dutch *Nieuw Amsterdam* and Cunard's second *Mauretania*. Other important ships of that immediate prewar period included the likes of Britain's *Andes* and *Dominion Monarch*, Holland's *Oranje*, the French *Pasteur*, and the *Stockholm* for Sweden. But as the war intensified in 1940 and 1941, these ships and all others were painted in grays, sailing in secret and delivering troops and supplies to every corner of the earth. United States Lines contributed three important, well known troopships: the *Wakefield* (ex-*Manhattan*), the *Mount Vernon* (ex-*Washington*), and the *West Point* (ex-*America*). They were heroic ships. Afterward, in the spring of 1946, with the war over, United States Lines attempted to resume its transatlantic passenger service. A chartered, partially-refitted liner, the *Argentina* of Moore-McCormack Lines, actually made the very first sailing between New York, Le Havre, and Southampton. The greatly refitted *America*, again bearing her original name, returned that November. Luxury service was restored for the company and, quite secretly, plans were well underway for a much larger liner—in fact, the most powerful and most advanced yet created. Some called her the "Super *America*."

The *America* was the first ship to be built under the U.S. Maritime Commission's mammoth plan to strengthen the nation's merchant navy with as many as 6,000 vessels, including passenger ships, freighters, tankers, and even tugs. At 33,900 tons, she was also the largest liner yet built in the United States. She was sleek, modern, fast, certainly very safe, but still smaller than Holland's brand new flagship, the 36,600-ton *Nieuw Amsterdam* or Cunard's second *Mauretania* at 35,600 tons. The Americans were cautious, remembering their great losses with the giant *Leviathan*, and also in view of the Depression years. Another consideration was that the greatest number of Atlantic travelers, including Americans themselves, often preferred European ships, where service and cuisine were thought to be better. Other than being the new flagship, the *America* was not out to break any great records. She was ceremoniously launched by Eleanor Roosevelt on August 31, 1939, as seen in this dramatic view of the Newport News Shipyard *(above)*. [Built by Newport News Shipbuilding & Dry Dock Company, Newport News, Virginia, 1940. 33,961 gross tons; 723 feet long; 94 feet wide. Steam turbines, twin screw. 1,046 passengers (516 first-class, 371 cabin-class, 159 tourist-class).]

Intended for the North Atlantic, the *America* was completed in July 1940 and immediately sent on a far safer routing: cruises to Bermuda, the Caribbean, and through the Panama Canal to California. But by early 1942, she and all other company passenger ships were in government hands, painted in anonymous grays, and even renamed: the *America* became USS *West Point*. She came under the Navy Department and her peacetime capacity increased from 1,046 to an official 8,145 in wartime, a number that was often exceeded. She was dispatched to ports all over the world: Rio, Bombay, Capetown, Sydney, San Francisco, and Marseilles. In February 1946, she took her last military trip from Manila to New York. During the war, the former *America*, along with the ex-*Manhattan* and ex-*Washington*, carried over one million military passengers. Immediately afterward, the *West Point* was returned to United States Lines, renamed *America*, and restored to her glorious self at Newport News, as seen in this imposing view from October 1946 *(opposite)*. She finally entered transatlantic commercial passenger service that November. For several months before then, United States Lines had made do with a chartered Moore-McCormack liner, the *Argentina*, which made a number of New York–Southampton sailings. Among her passengers at this time were the Duke and Duchess of Windsor, who returned from a wartime posting in the Bahamas to their home in Paris. Later, the Windsors would become the most celebrated passengers to sail with United States Lines.

As mentioned, the *America*, the third teammate to the popular *Manhattan* and *Washington* of 1932–33, had a somewhat larger design closely inspired by another design of William Francis Gibbs, the Grace Line's *Santa Rosa* and her three identical sisters. Although far smaller at a mere 9,900 tons, their exteriors are noticeably similar to that of the new United States Lines' flagship. In particular, the finned, forward funnel on the Grace ships was carried further aboard the *America*. There seems to have been one mistake, however—in fact, a repeated mistake. When first built, both the *Manhattan* and *Washington* had squat, small stacks, but these were soon raised to reduce the amounts of smoke and soot coming down on the aft passenger decks. When first completed, the *America* also had very low funnels, as seen in this view dated March 11, 1940, when she was still fitting out (*opposite, top*). Following her sea trials that spring and early summer, the low-standing funnels proved impractical and were quickly raised.

C. M. Squarey, the noted British appraiser of passenger ships, wrote of the *America* in 1950, "I pay this liner the compliment, by my code, of saying that she has not got glamour; rather has she the greater asset of irresistible attraction based on sophisticated charm. She blends very nicely restraint with progress; she incorporates a modern approach to problems with just the right touch of respect for the older school." She was often said to have been the most beautiful of all American-flag passenger liners, and as handsome on the outside as she was on the inside. "She was a very charming ship and a very cozy ship," recalled maritime historian Everett Viez, who sailed the *America* several times. Her first-class restaurant (*opposite, bottom*) was one of her finest spaces.

For a short time in the late 1940s, the *America* was repainted with an experimental gray hull (formerly black). Since she was being used for occasional winter cruises from New York to the Caribbean, seen here anchored off San Juan, Puerto Rico in February 1950 (*above*), the lighter color was thought to reduce the warm temperatures onboard. It soon reverted to black, however, due to the difficulty of maintaining the gray paint. The *America* had partial air-conditioning, limited to her public rooms.

Assisting the *America* for a short time in the late 1940s were eight former wartime transports. They were made over by the government, but with comparatively austere accommodations for up to 900 one-class passengers. After President Truman authorized the Displaced Persons Program in late 1945, a steady flow of Europeans began to come westbound. The first group, about 800 in all and most of them from Nazi concentration camps, left Bremerhaven for New York in May 1946 onboard the *Marine Flasher*, which was then chartered to United States Lines. Two days later, a sailing by the *Marine Perch* followed. Afterward, six other ships were chartered: *Marine Marlin*, *Marine Falcon*, *Marine Jumper*, *Marine Tiger*, *Marine Shark*, and the specially named *Ernie Pyle*. Later, these ships also carried war brides, students, and even some of the first budget tourists headed for Europe. They sailed to Southampton, Le Havre, Antwerp, Bremerhaven, Oslo, Copenhagen, and Gdynia. By the end of 1949, however, the ships were phased out and their charters can-

celled. Here we see one of their identical sisters, the *Marine Lynx* (*opposite, top*). Most of them were eventually mothballed and later rebuilt as freighters and enlarged containerships before being scrapped by the 1980s. [Built by Kaiser Company, Company, Vancouver, Washington, 1945. 12,420 gross tons; 523 feet long; 71 feet wide. Steam turbines, single screw. Service speed 16 knots. 3,485 troops as built.]

Like most great liners that plied the North Atlantic, the *America* often contended with less-than-ideal weather conditions. In this view (*opposite, bottom*), from January 24, 1948, the ship's diligent photographer captured this storm-tossed scene.

Each winter, the *America* returned to her birthplace, the Newport News Shipyard, for her annual overhaul and special repairs. In this view dated April 2, 1950 (*above*), she is in one of the big graving docks as the early steel skeleton of another ship emerges in the adjacent graving dock. The new vessel is, of course, her future running mate, the mighty *United States*.

The *America* was especially well known in New York and remained popular long after the first appearance of the bigger, faster, more modern *United States*. The older ship is seen here in one of New York's classic gatherings of great ocean liners (*above*). In a view dated April 24, 1957, from top to bottom, are the *Berlin* (just sailing), North German Lloyd; the *Queen Federica*, National Hellenic American Line; *Media* (mostly obscured), *Queen Mary*, and the freighter *Alsatia*, all Cunard; *Liberté* and *Ile de France*, both French Line; United States Lines' *American Scout* and the *America*; the *Giulio Cesare*, Italian Line; and the *Constitution*, American Export Lines.

Evidently, after the highly successful maiden voyage of the *United States* in July 1952, plans turned toward a possible replacement for the *America*. There was subsequent talk of a 40,000-tonner that would have a high service speed of 30 knots or more. Although smaller by some 12,000 tons, such a new vessel would cost $110 million, or $30 million more than the *United States*. Washington became less and less interested in underwriting new liners, however, and so eventually the plan was dropped. The *America*'s port bridge wing is seen here (*opposite, top*) just as she arrives on the south side of Pier 86. The enormous forward funnel

of the *United States* is in the background. The photo was shot in the earliest light of day.

By the early 1960s, the great passenger-ship lines began to struggle. Simply, there were fewer and fewer customers in this, the new jet age. American liners suffered from another major problem: they were the most expensive liners to operate in the world. In September 1963, there were some racially-tainted labor problems among some of the *America*'s crew members, such that her next sailing and several subsequent voyages were canceled, and the ship laid-up temporarily. "It was all a prelude to the end of that ship, to the *United States* and to the entire U.S.-flag passenger fleet," remembered one former officer. "Time was running out—too few passengers and too many costly crew members."

In the fall of 1964, the *America* was sold to a Greek company called the Chandris Lines. Heavily involved in the Europe-Australia migrant business, as well as the around-the-world tourist trade, the ship was refitted as the *Australis* (*opposite, bottom*). With her capacity was more than doubled, from 1,046 to 2,258, a second, highly profitable life of continuous three-month-long trips around the world began.

The *Australis* was sold in 1977, becoming the first and only member of the short-lived Venture Cruise Lines. Renamed *America*, her short three-, four-, and five-day cruises out of New York could not have been less successful. With her owners bankrupt, she was seized by U.S. marshals and resold to Chandris, who repaired and restyled her (removing the forward "dummy" funnel) as the *Italis* for European cruising. Soon, however, she was laid-up in the backwaters near Piraeus, Greece, where she fell into considerable decay. There were many reports and rumors of projected future plans for her: a Montreal hotel, a Australian marina, a trade fair ship in China, and even a floating prison in Galveston, Texas. Occasionally, there was news of possibly bringing her back to New York as a moored hotel ship. This view *(above)*, from her long-neglected starboard sundeck, dates from October 13, 1992.

Nothing came to pass until 1992, when the *America* was sold to Thai investors, who wanted to remake her as a hotel, the *American Star*, moored near Bangkok. Unfortunately, she encountered a fierce storm north of the Canary Islands while under tow, en route to the East via the South African Cape in January 1994. Pitched onto the rocks, she later broke in half and was abandoned *(below)*. The aft end subsequently separated, drifted into the sea, and then sank. At the time of writing, only 400 feet of the forward part of the once-great *America* remains. Though she deserves better, the *America* was destined for a very sad ending.

CHAPTER III

~

Workhorses on Water:
Cargo Ships of United States Lines

United States Lines had the biggest freighter fleet under the American flag by the late '40s through the '50s. In 1950, a peak period, it had over fifty cargo ships. "United States Lines' freighters greatly helped in the rebuilding of Europe just after the war and into the early 1950s," said the late Joseph Mazzotta, who served as the U.S. Coast Guard's Commandant of the Port of New York. "Alone, United States Lines would have four or five ships sailing every Friday afternoon for British and North European ports. Sometimes, one, two, or even three ships would follow one another and appear to be a train. Of course, they were easily noticed with their red, white, and blue funnel colors.

"They carried all the varied American manufactured goods to Europe in those days, including lots of automobiles. They also transported lots of food and grain," added Captain Mazzotta. "U.S. Lines occupied more piers then than any other shipping company using New York. They were the sole occupants of the Chelsea Piers, Numbers 59, 60, 61, and 62, which stretched from West 17th to West 22nd streets on Manhattan's West Side. They also had Pier 74 at West 34th Street, and the larger Pier 86 at West 46th Street. In Staten Island, they used Pier 11 in Stapleton and, for the frequent large military cargoes they also carried, their freighters were often berthed at the big Army Terminal over at 57th Street in Brooklyn, or alternately at the Bayonne Military Ocean Terminal in New Jersey. Sometimes, as I remember it from the late 1940s, a U.S. Lines freighter might have to wait at anchor in the Lower Bay, in the Narrows, for an available berth up at Chelsea or elsewhere. Sometimes, they went instead to the Bethlehem Steel Shipyard over in Hoboken or to Todd's Yard in Brooklyn for some maintenance and light repairs, even though they were still loaded with inbound freight. They were busy, almost hectic, times, but like all other practical shipowners, they always attempted to avoid the weekends, which had huge stevedoring overtime charges. They always tried to have all ships cleared and away by Friday evenings."

Changeover to the then-new containerized method of cargo transport in the 1960s did away with the old-fashioned break-bulk freighters. Increasingly larger containerships became a part of United States Lines. It also meant a shift away from conventional terminals such as the Chelsea Piers in Manhattan and, with the need for open spaces to marshal containers, to larger areas in more distant New Jersey and on Staten Island. After 1969 and the withdrawal of the *United States*, container shipping was the mainstay of United States Lines. An increasingly competitive business, and one greatly affected by worldwide economic trading and financial conditions, the company built no less than a dozen mega-containerships in 1984 to maintain a strong competitive edge. Unfortunately, the ships were designed with errors, namely too little power and, therefore, slow service speeds. Foreign-flag companies snatched away the bulk of the container business, and so the company continued to lose money until, in November 1986, it suddenly and dramatically slipped into bankruptcy. In virtually a single afternoon, the 64-year-old United States Lines was gone. The twelve big containerships were later auctioned to repay the defunct firm's outstanding debts.

∾ AMERICAN JURIST

On the eve of the maiden arrival of the *United States* in the winter of 1951–52, United States Lines had over fifty freighters flying its house flag. There were six Victory ships: the *American Attorney, American Counselor, American Defender, American Judge, American Jurist (opposite, top)*, and *American Lawyer*. Along with the famous Liberty ships, these "Victories," as they were dubbed, were the workhorses of the final years of the Second World War. In modern methods of prefabrication, these deep-sea vessels could be constructed in days, rather than weeks or months. Altogether, there were over 500 Victory ships and more than 2,700 Liberty ships. But while the "Liberties" were slightly smaller and much slower (a mere 11 knots at best), the Victory ships were especially designed with an eye toward commercial operation after the war. Many were used commercially by other American shipowners beginning in the late 1940s, while others went under foreign flags, some of which were converted to passenger ships. The Dutch, for example, refitted three of the "Victories" with as many as 800 passenger berths.

These United States Lines' Victory ships, which primarily sailed the Northern European run, were phased out by the mid-1950s and sold off. The *American Jurist*, for example, which had been completed in October 1945 as the *Parkersburg Victory* until transferred to United States Lines in 1948, became the *Federal Jurist* in 1956. She was sold to foreign-flag owners a year later and began to take on a long list of successive names: *Wang Pioneer, Interocean, Hercules Victory, Hermina*, and *Tia Sylvia* before being broken-up on Taiwan in 1970. [Built by Bethlehem-Fairfield Shipyard, Inc., Baltimore, Maryland, 1945. 7,600 gross tons; 455 feet long; 62 feet wide. Steam turbines, single screw. Service speed 16 knots. 12 passengers.]

∾ AMERICAN BUILDER

United States Lines had about two dozen of the C2-Class of conventional freighters in the early 1950s. These ships, such as the *American Builder*, seen here on a late afternoon departure with Lower Manhattan in the background (*opposite, bottom*), were outbound for at least two European ports of call. It was one of 250 freighter voyages made by the company in 1952. Along the American East Coast, in addition to New York, these ships called at Boston, Philadelphia, Baltimore, and Norfolk. Abroad, their regular ports of call included Dublin, Liverpool, Glasgow, London, Le Havre, Antwerp, Rotterdam, Bremen, and Hamburg. There were also occasional military cargo voyages to the ports of Rota and Cadiz in Spain. [Built by Moore Dry Dock Company, Oakland, California, 1945. 8,330 gross tons; 459 feet long; 63 feet wide. Steam turbines, single screw. Service speed 16 knots. 12 passengers.]

∾ PIONEER GLEN

The company ran another two dozen or so slightly different C2-Class freighters. Some had the customary "American" prefix names and were used on the Atlantic; others used *Pioneer* names for the subsidiary American Pioneer Line services to the Far East and the South Pacific. The *Pioneer Glen (above)* was assigned to the latter service, sailing from New York to the likes of Papeete, Brisbane, and Sydney, with calls en route at Norfolk, Savannah, Houston, and New Orleans before passing through the Panama Canal. There was a sailing every two weeks in the 1950s. The *Pioneer Glen*, completed for the Maritime Commission in the fall of 1945 as the *Rapid*, joined United States Lines two years later and was immediately assigned to the American Pioneer division. She was sold to Farrell Lines in 1965 and became their *Australian Galaxy*. She was scrapped on Taiwan in 1970. [Built by North Carolina Shipbuilding Company, Wilmington, North Carolina, 1945. 8,228 gross tons; 459 feet long; 63 feet wide. Steam turbines, single screw. Service speed 16 knots. 12 passengers.]

∾ PIONEER GEM

United States Lines' freighters, including the *Pioneer Gem*, seen loading cargo at Pier 61 in New York (*above*), were very popular with passengers. Many travelers preferred the longer time at sea, as well as the casual atmosphere of these ships. In the early 1950s, fares from New York were approximately $150 to London, $175 to Bremen, $350 to Sydney, and $500 to Yokohama. Round-trip voyages to the Far East on American Pioneer ships might have lasted as long as ten weeks. [Built by North Carolina Shipbuilding Company, Wilmington, North Carolina, 1945. 8,229 gross tons; 459 feet long; 63 feet wide. Steam turbines, single screw. Service speed 16 knots. 12 passengers.]

∾ AMERICAN CLIPPER

America's Freedom Bell, on tour through Europe in 1950, is seen here after being loaded aboard the freighter *American Clipper* at Pier 62 in New York (*opposite*). The liner *America* is seen just across the slip, berthed at Pier 61.

～ **Winter in New York**

Four United States Lines' ships are captured in this winter photo from 1960 (*overleaf*). The *United States* is outbound, having just sailed at noon from Pier 86, at the foot of West 46th Street. She passes two inbound company freighters: the *American Shipper* (left) is headed for Pier 86, while the *Pioneer Land* (right) is just beginning to make a swing toward Pier 74, at the foot of West 34th Street. A fourth ship, the *Pioneer Gem*, is already docked at Pier 74.

⌐ PIONEER MINX

For the American Pioneer Line service to the Far East—Manila, Hong Kong, Taipei, Pusan, Kobe, and Yokohama—United States Lines ran eight of the largest, fastest freighters afloat in the 1950s. They belonged to a group of thirty-five or so Mariner Class ships and were added to the company's fleet in 1955–56. "Ships like the *Pioneer Minx* and her sisters were actually owned by the government, but leased to United States Lines," noted Captain Ed Squire, a onetime staff member. "Washington especially wanted them on the Far East and in particular sailing to Japan as postwar symbols of American might and technology. It was a great period, the 1950s, for the company as well. United States Lines not only owned the fastest and most advanced passenger liner afloat, but the largest and fastest cargo liners as well."

The *Pioneer Minx (above)*, first completed as the *Gopher Mariner*, was rebuilt in 1970 as an enlarged containership, the 15,864-ton *American Leader*. She sailed for United States Lines until broken-up on Taiwan in the mid-1980s. [Built by Bethlehem Steel Company, Sparrows Point, Maryland, 1953. 8,964 gross tons; 564 feet long; 76 feet wide. Steam turbines, single screw. Service speed 20 knots. 12 passengers.]

⌐ AMERICAN CHALLENGER

New, more advanced freighters were built by United States Lines beginning in the early 1960s. Most were later modified to carry containers. As built, the *American Challenger* and her seven sisters took a few small, 20-foot containers on their decks in addition to the traditional stowed cargo. Seen here in 1965, the Chelsea Piers themselves were being rebuilt and modernized to suit the new demands of containerized cargo shipping. Pier 62 was demolished entirely and remade as an open space for stacking containers. On this wintry afternoon *(opposite)*, the *Challenger* is docked in the foreground, with the *United States* headed downriver and another U.S.-flag liner, the *Constitution* of American Export Lines, sitting high in dry dock at the Bethlehem Steel Shipyard in Hoboken. Soon after she was completed, the *American Challenger* claimed the transatlantic speed record for cargo ships with an average of 24.11 knots. Consequently, United States Lines had the fastest liner as well as the fastest freighter on the North Atlantic. [Built by Newport News Shipbuilding & Dry Dock Company, Newport News, Virginia, 1962. 11,105 gross tons; 561 feet long; 75 feet wide. Steam turbines, single screw. Service speed 20 knots.]

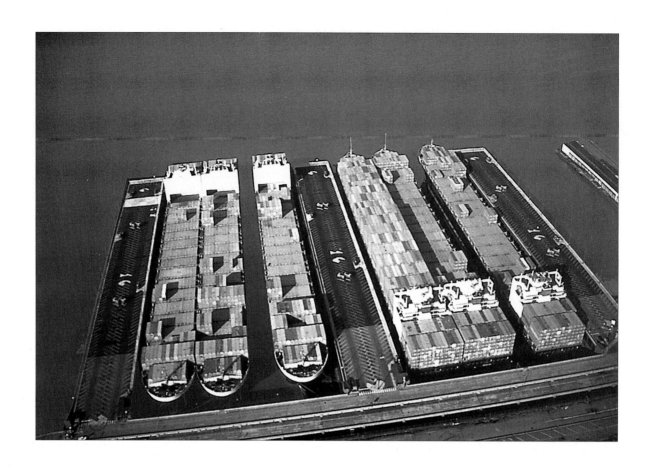

❧ Waiting for Work

The trend for bigger containerships begun in the 1970s prompted United States Lines to order the biggest containerships yet—no less than twelve 57,000-tonners from a South Korean shipyard in 1984–85. Costing altogether $570 million, the Koreans financed 80% of that amount. The first of them, the *American New York*, was commissioned in July 1984. Known as the *American New York* class, each was named for a different state and was based at a specially enlarged container facility at Howland Hook in New York. They were created for continuous, eighty-four-day around-the-world service with a sailing from New York each week. However, these ships, with a capacity of 2,228 forty-foot containers each, were built on a tight budget and, in a great miscalculation, were highly under-powered and therefore sailed at a slow speed. They could manage a mere 16 knots, which compared unfavorably to the 20–25 knot speeds of their European and Asian competitors. As a result, United States Lines lost cargo contracts and slipped deeper into the red. "In the end we were carrying mostly used paper, then an American export," recalled a head office staff member. "We lost the really the valuable, very important cargos." Headquartered at Cranford, New Jersey since 1979, United States Lines was finally declared bankrupt (with debts of $1.7 billion and an annual loss in 1985 of close to $67 million) and closed down in November 1986. Its ships were seized by the banks and other creditors, laid-up for a time (as six of them are seen here *(above)*, in the winter of 1987, at New York's Passenger Ship Terminal), and then auctioned off. Most of them were eventually sold to Sea-Land Service, also American-based, and some of those were later re-engined. [Built by Daewoo Shipbuilding & Heavy Industries Limited, Koje, South Korea, 1984. 57,076 gross tons; 950 feet long; 105 feet wide. Diesels, twin screw. Service speed 16 knots.]

CHAPTER IV

⁓

Other Ships Flying the Stars & Stripes

In the 1950s, it was still something of a boom period for passenger ships, even those under the costly, labor-troubled, strike-prone U.S. flag. Travel by ship was still very popular and was not seriously affected by airline competition—at least, not until the first appearance of far faster jet aircraft in October 1958. Ironically, on an inbound voyage off the Statue of Liberty, the *United States* had just logged her millionth mile. After the jets arrived, operating passenger ships did not just slow down—they came to an almost abrupt halt. The Americans were among the first to be hit. The 1960s were especially harsh, such that by 1972, there were only four passenger ships still flying the red, white, and blue. The last of these would be gone within six years.

Earlier, in 1952, at the time of the maiden voyage of the *United States*, however, one could still travel to nearly all four corners of the world on an American passenger ship. Altogether, there were some forty ships that were considered passenger ships, rather than freighters, because they carried more than the maximum of twelve people. There were the big liners, smaller ones, and combination passenger-cargo ships that generally carried between fifty to one hundred travelers. There were also peacetime troopships, which were civilian-manned vessels under the Military Sea Transportation Service (MSTS). These transports not only carried troops, but their families and other government personnel as well. Some of them also made sailings with displaced persons, refugees, and survivors from the Nazi death camps, and often these west-bound voyages to New York from northern Europe were handled by United States Lines. Additionally, the U.S. government maintained as many as nine "mothball fleets" in the early '50s, with over thirty former passenger ships and idle troop transports at anchor in 1952. The largest of these included the 24,000-ton *Manhattan* and *Washington*, formerly of United States Lines, along with the *Edmund B. Alexander* (formerly the *America*) built in 1905 and also once operated by United States Lines. Another noted, idle passenger ship was the *Thomas H. Barry*, formerly the cruise ship *Oriente*, built in 1930 and twin sister to the ill-fated *Morro Castle*.

In the early 1950s, Moore McCormack Lines had three large liners operating a route down the east coast of South America, while the Grace Line had two liners and nine combo ships running to the Caribbean and the South American Pacific coast. United Fruit still had five "banana boats" that carried passengers on cruiselike sailings to Central America. The Panama Line had a trio of ships trading between New York, the Caribbean, and the Canal Zone. Out on the West Coast, Matson was running one big liner to Hawaii and back, while American President Lines ran two liners and two combo ships—the former pair to Far East ports and the latter on three-

month trips around the world. From the U.S. Gulf, the Delta Line operated three combo ships to South America while the Alcoa Company also had three combo vessels that remained in Caribbean waters. The two largest liners, apart from the *America* and the *United States*, were American Export Lines' then-brand-new *Independence* and *Constitution*, which sailed between New York and western Mediterranean ports. One former transport, the *La Guardia*, had been converted to commercial passenger status, but proved a troublesome and expensive ship to operate. After a stint with American Export on the Atlantic, she reverted to trooping service, sailing under the management of United States Lines in 1952. Her career would change often, however, including subsequent phases for two American passenger firms, the short-lived Hawaiian-Textron Lines and American President Lines.

In 1952, Washington was still looking favorably on passenger ships for both trade and potential military use. Shipowners were still enthusiastic as well: United States Lines still wanted a replacement for the *America*, possibly a ship of 40,000 tons; American Export wanted a third liner to join their *Independence* and *Constitution*; and American President Lines was planning a 43,000-ton, modified version of the *United States* that would be called *President Washington*. None of these ideas ever came to pass. Future tonnage was rather conservative: three high-speed Mariner Class freighters would be converted to liners, and both the Grace and Moore-McCormack Lines would each build a pair of new, but moderately-sized passenger ships. A special project, the nuclear-powered *Savannah*, which had sixty passenger berths, was added in 1962 and operated for a short time by American Export Lines. In the early '60s, Grace added a new quartet of combination passenger-container ships, but these were, in fact, the last new passenger ships to be built in an American shipyard or for an American shipowner. Two 72,000-ton cruise ships were on order by 1999 for American Classic Voyages, a cruise company, and were to sail a Hawaiian route under their United States Lines' banner, a name bought from the defunct company. In October 2001, however, American Classic collapsed, and the orders for the two new ships were canceled. Later, Miami-based Norwegian Cruise Lines, then the third-largest cruise operator in North America, bought both unfinished ships. Once seaworthy, the first was towed in November 2002 to Bremerhaven for final completion and is due out in the spring of 2004. It is yet unnamed as we went to press, but will cruise under the U.S. flag. In this age of a multi-billion dollar American cruise industry, long dominated by foreign-flag ships, the American flag will be seen aboard high-standard ocean liners once more. American passenger ship history will continue!

31

∾ BRAZIL

New York–headquartered Moore-McCormack Lines operated three liners on thirty-eight-day round-trip itineraries to ports along the East Coast of South America: a stop at Trinidad before steaming to Rio de Janeiro, Santos, Montevideo, and Buenos Aires. The *Brazil* (**above**) and her two running mates, the *Argentina* and *Uruguay*, were formerly a part of United States Lines, belonging to their Panama Pacific Line subsidiary and having been the *Virginia*, *Pennsylvania*, and *California*, respectively. They proved too big for the intercoastal trade between New York and California, and so were refitted in 1938 as the "Good Neighbor Ships" for Moore-McCormack. Used as troopers during the Second World War, the trio revived their Latin American service in the late '40s. Eleven days from New York to Rio was priced from $500 for first-class accommodations. [Built by Newport News Shipbuilding & Dry Dock Company, Newport News, Virginia, 1928. 20,683 gross tons; 613 feet long; 80 feet feet wide. Steam turbo-electric engines, twin screw. 515 passengers (356 first-class, 159 cabin-class).]

∾ LURLINE

Matson Line of San Francisco built three quite exceptional luxury sister ships in the early '30s: the *Mariposa*, *Monterey*, and *Lurline*. Only the *Lurline* (**opposite, top**) returned to American commercial service following World War II, however, making regular five-day voyages between San Francisco, Los Angeles, and Honolulu. She was a great favorite on the West Coast. Her sisters, laid-up in 1946 because of the high costs of converting them back to liners, were revived later: the *Mariposa* became the *Homeric* in 1954 for the European company, Home Lines; the *Monterey* was refitted by Matson in 1957 and began sailing as the *Matsonia*. In 1963, when the original *Lurline* was sold to Greek interests, the *Matsonia* took on that very popular name until she, too, was sold to a Greek firm in 1970. When she sank off the South African coast in October 2000, under tow for demolition in India, she was sixty-eight years old. [Built by Bethlehem Steel Company, Quincy, Massachusetts, 1932. 18,564 gross tons; 631 feet long; 79 feet wide. Steam turbines, twin screw. Service speed 20 knots. 761 all-first-class passengers.]

∾ PUERTO RICO

A smaller American passenger ship that ran until the early 1950s was the *Puerto Rico* (**opposite, bottom**), seen here in dry dock at Bethlehem Steel's Hoboken, New Jersey shipyard. Operated by the Bull Line, she sailed on eleven-day round-trips between New York, San Juan, and Ciudad Trujillo. She had sailed a similar run in her earlier days as the *Borinquen* for the New York and Porto Rico Line. Bull bought her in 1949. However, in addition to the airline competition factor, one-ship liner operations were rarely successful. The *Puerto Rico* was out of service within four years and was sold to the Swiss-owned Arosa Line. She became their *Arosa Star* and, in 1959, was sold and renamed *Bahama Star*, becoming one of the first year-round cruise ships based at Miami. [Built by Bethlehem Steel Company, Quincy, Massachusetts, 1931. 7,114 gross tons; 429 feet long; 60 feet wide. Steam turbines, single screw. Service speed 15 knots. 200 all-first-class passengers.]

◌ SANTA ROSA

Designed by William Francis Gibbs and clearly a prelude to the far larger *America* and *United States*, a quartet of sister ships was built by the Grace Line in the early 1930s for its Caribbean and South American routes from both U.S. East and West Coast ports. They were the *Santa Rosa* (shown here outbound at New York, **opposite, top**), *Santa Paula*, *Santa Elena*, and *Santa Lucia*. After the latter two were sunk in the Second World War, the *Rosa* and the *Paula* restored the company's twelve-day round-trip passenger and cruise service between New York, Aruba, La Guaira, Curacao, and Cartagena. Full cruise rates began at $435. Replaced by new liners of the same names in 1958, they were later sold to a Greek shipowner. The *Rosa* became the *Athinai* and the *Paula* was renamed the *Acropolis*. [Built by Federal Shipbuilding & Dry Dock Company, Kearny, New Jersey, 1932. 9,135 gross tons; 508 feet long; 72 feet wide. Steam turbines, twin screw. Service speed 20 knots. 225 all-first-class passengers.]

◌ QUIRIGUA

The United Fruit Company, otherwise known as "the Great White Fleet" and noted for their gleaming banana boats, had six passenger-cargo ships in service to Caribbean and Central American ports after World War II. The *Quirigua* (shown here, **opposite, bottom**, on February 18, 1947, as she reentered postwar commercial service), the *Veragua*, the *Antigua*, and the *Talamanca* handled the business out of New York, while two other sisters, the *Chiriqui* and *Jamaica*, ran from New Orleans. Full cruise as well as port-to-port services were available. The three-and-a-half-day run from New York to Havana, for example, was very popular in the late '40s and early '50s, and cost $100. Airline competition, however, caused United Fruit to concentrate only on twelve-passenger freighters, and so the New York passenger run was phased out in 1953 and the New Orleans

service by 1957. The structures of these passenger ships were cut down and thereafter they sailed purely as freighters. [Built by Bethlehem Steel Company, Quincy, Massachusetts, 1932. 6,982 gross tons; 447 feet long; 60 feet wide. Steam turbo-electric, twin screw. Service speed 18 knots. 100 one-class passengers.]

◌ CRISTOBAL

Three of the most modern American passenger ships belonged to the Panama Line, an offshoot of the U.S. government-owned Panama Railroad Company. Named *Ancon*, *Cristobal* (seen here in later years at New Orleans, **above**), and *Panama*, they were built just before the Second World War began in Europe, in 1939, and were created to provide weekly departures between New York and the Canal Zone with passenger, general cargo, provisions, and mail. Their smart exteriors included light gray-colored hulls, silver-coated masts and lifeboats, and a large buff funnel encircled by triple silver strands. Internally, their decor was entrusted to Raymond Loewy, the so-called "king of streamline," and the result was a high form of Art Deco: simple overall decor, steel tube chairs, and stainless handrails. Amenities included a lido area and small pool, air conditioning in the restaurant (something of a novelty for the late '30s), and a private bathroom for each stateroom. Some cabins had the added novelty of shared, glass-enclosed verandahs. After the war, they resumed their services, including fourteen-day cruises priced from $330. The *Panama* was sold to American President Lines in 1957 and became the *President Hoover*, while the *Ancon* and *Cristobal* closed out the New York passenger service in 1961. [Built by Bethlehem Steel Company, Quincy, Massachusetts, 1939. 9,978 gross tons; 493 feet long; 64 feet wide. Steam turbines, twin screw. Service speed 17½ knots. 216 all-first-class passengers.]

∿ GENERAL WILLIAM WEIGEL

Beginning in 1944, as part of the great American shipbuilding effort during World War II, when over 6,000 deep-sea ships were built, the U.S. government ordered several series of troopships to deliver more forces overseas and hasten the conflict's end. Some of these were even designed to continue trooping once the war was over, while others were intended to be adapted for commercial service for the American President, United States, Grace, Moore-McCormack, and Farrell Lines. The largest of these ships belonged to the P2-S2-R2 series and were topped off by very large funnels. The *General William Weigel* was one of eleven sister ships in this class and is seen here **(right)** arriving at Pier 1 of the Brooklyn Army Terminal. Family members and friends hold signs of the names of inbound soldier-passengers. Beginning in 1949, these troopships were assigned to the Military Sea Transportation Service (MSTS) for contin-ued government service carrying troops and dependent families. The ships were civilian-manned and sailed the Atlantic (usually between New York and Southampton, Bremerhaven, or Rota in Spain) as well as the Pacific (from San Francisco or Seattle to Yokohama, Kobe, Pusan, Okinawa, Manila, Subic Bay, Guam, and Honolulu). [Built by Federal Shipbuilding & Dry Dock Company, Kearny, New Jersey, 1945. 17,800 gross tons; 622 feet long; 75 feet wide. Steam turbines, twin screw. Service speed 19 knots. 6,000 troops in wartime; reduced to 4,000 and later 2,000 in peacetime.]

∾ PRESIDENT POLK

Beginning in 1946, American President Lines ran two fine passenger-cargo liners, the *President Monroe* and the *President Polk*—seen here during an inbound call at Boston (*opposite, top*)—on a popular one-hundred-day around-the-world service that had fares beginning at $2,990. Their routing took passengers to New York, Cristobal, Balboa, Acapulco, Los Angeles, San Francisco, Honolulu, Yokohama, Kobe, Hong Kong, Saigon, Singapore, Penang, Cochin, Bombay, Karachi, Port Suez, Port Said, Alexandria, Naples, Marseilles, Genoa, Leghorn, and then back to New York. During the New York stays of ten or so days, the ships made so-called "coastal swings" for cargo at Boston, Philadelphia, Baltimore, and Norfolk. These twin ships were replaced by twelve-berth freighters in 1965 and then sold off to foreign-flag shipowners. [Built by Newport News Shipbuilding & Dry Dock Company, Newport News, Virginia, 1940. 9,225 gross tons; 492 feet long; 70 feet wide. Steam turbines, single screw. Service speed 16½ knots. 96 all-first-class passengers.]

∾ LEILANI

Soon after the war ended, plans were made to convert several of these large troopships into commercial liners, including at least two for United States Lines' North Atlantic service between New York, Southampton, Le Havre, and Bremerhaven. Being heavy ships (with extra-thick hull plating that caused drag and, therefore, much greater fuel consumption), they were not necessarily viable propositions from a private shipowner's viewpoint. In fact, only one ship, the *General W. P. Richardson*, was converted in 1948–49.

Renamed *La Guardia*, she was used in American Export's New York-Mediterranean passenger service, but for only three years and with only minimal success. She was returned to the government and used as a trooper (for a time under United States Lines' operation between New York, Southampton, and Bremerhaven as well as to Caribbean bases) before being further refitted as the *Leilani* on a San Francisco–Honolulu service for the short-lived Hawaiian-Textron Lines. She is seen here (*opposite, bottom*) arriving in New York in January 1957 on her special maiden voyage to the West Coast via Panama. Still unprofitable, she became American President Lines' *President Roosevelt* in 1962. [Built by Federal Shipbuilding & Dry Dock Company, Kearny, New Jersey, 1944. 18,298 gross tons; 622 feet long; 75 feet wide. Steam turbines, twin screw. Service speed 19 knots. 650 single-class passengers.]

∾ OCEAN EXPLORER I

After serving as the *General W. P. Richardson*, *La Guardia*, *Leilani*, and then as the *President Roosevelt* under the U.S. flag, this ship was sold to the Greek-flag Chandris Lines in 1970 and became their *Atlantis*. Through further sales, beginning in 1972, it was then renamed *Emerald Seas*, *Fantastica*, *Funtastica*, *Terrifica*, *Sun Fiesta*, *Sapphire Seas*, and *Ocean Explorer I* (as she is seen here, *above*, in early 2001, laid-up in Eleusis Bay in Greece). She last sailed as a cruise ship in 1999 and, in May 2001, was chartered for use as a floating hotel in Genoa during the World Economic Summit. Still afloat, she is one of the very last of the American troopships built in World War II.

⌒ GENERAL EDWIN D. PATRICK

The second series of large troopships, the slightly smaller P2-SE2-R1 type, were designed especially for transpacific service. Ten were ordered, but only eight were completed, with the other two being sold to American President Lines and completed as the liners *President Cleveland* and *President Wilson*. After the war, these ships, such as the *General Edwin D. Patrick* (*above*), sailed the Pacific as well as the Atlantic. One of the last surviving members of this class, the *General Hugh J. Gaffey*, was used as a floating barracks before being scrapped in 2000. [Built by Bethlehem-Alameda Shipyard Inc., Alameda, California, 1944. Approximately 16,000 gross tons; 609 feet long; 75 feet wide. Steam turbo-electric, twin screw. Service speed 19 knots. Approximately 5,000 troops during wartime; reduced to 2,000 in peacetime.]

⌒ GENERAL LE ROY ELTINGE

There were thirty ships in the engines-aft C4 troopship class, including the *General Le Roy Eltinge*, shown here leaving Bayonne, New Jersey (*opposite, top*) on a special emergency voyage with supplies, food, and medical technicians for the troubled Belgian Congo in 1960. Functional ships in every respect, this class had been rather hurriedly built by Henry J. Kaiser's special wartime shipyard at Richmond, California. Carrying as many as 3,000 troops during the war, they were used well into the 1950s by MSTS, as well as to carry refugees and dependents on voyages, often under the management of the United States and American President Lines. Mostly laid-up by the late 1950s, many were even-

tually sold off and rebuilt as freighters, heavy-lift ships, and as enlarged containerships. The *Eltinge* finished her career as the freighter *Robert E. Lee* before being broken-up in Taiwan in 1980. [Built by the Kaiser Company Inc., Richmond, California, 1944. 10,600 gross tons; 523 feet long; 72 feet wide. Steam turbines, twin screw. Service speed 17 knots. Up to 3,000 troops in wartime; over 2,000 in peacetime.]

⌒ GEORGE W. GOETHALS

Four postwar troopships had originally been designed as combination passenger-cargo ships for a subsidiary of United States Lines, the American Merchant Line. The ships were planned for the New York–London run, carrying 165 all-first-class passengers each, and were named *American Merchant, American Banker, American Shipper,* and *American Farmer*. But soon after their construction started in 1941, they were taken over by the U.S. government and renamed. The *George W. Goethals* (*opposite, bottom*), the intended *American Merchant*, was redesigned to carry up to 2,000 troops during the World War II, but was modified in 1946 to transport up to 450 military spouses and children. Often used in MSTS's New York to San Juan or Guantanamo Bay service, she was decommissioned in 1960 and dismantled in Spain a decade later. [Built by Ingalls Shipbuilding Corporation, Pascagoula, Mississippi, 1941. 11,900 gross tons; 492 feet long; 70 feet wide. Steam turbines, single screw. Service speed 17 knots. 452 passengers in peacetime.]

DEL NORTE

The New Orleans–based Delta Line added three fine combo liners to their services in 1946. Known as the *Del Mar, Del Norte* (shown here at New Orleans, ***opposite, top***), and *Del Sud*, they had rather unusual profiles: flat dummy stacks, with the actual exhausts working through the twin pipes just behind. Used in a service to ports along the east coast of South America, they are notable as the first commercial ships to be equipped with radar. [Built by Ingalls Shipbuilding Corporation, Pascagoula, Mississippi, 1946. 10,073 gross tons; 495 feet long; 70 feet wide. Steam turbines, single screw. Service speed 16½ knots. 119 all-first-class passengers.]

AFRICAN ENTERPRISE

Another shipowner headquartered in New York, Farrell Lines ran two splendid combination ships to ports in South & East Africa (Capetown, Port Elizabeth, Durban, Lourenco Marques, and Beira). Used by business travelers and tourists alike, the *African Endeavor* and *African Enterprise* (***opposite, bottom***) provided an almost yacht-like service on these impeccably run ships. [Built by

Bethlehem Steel Company, Sparrows Point, Maryland, 1940. 7,997 gross tons; 491 feet long; 66 feet wide. Steam turbines, single screw. Service speed 16½ knots. 82 all-first-class passengers.]

SANTA BARBARA

Immediately following the war, the Grace Line added no less than nine brand-new combination ships for its Caribbean and South American west coast routes. The first six were primarily for the longer voyages and were named *Santa Barbara* (seen here departing from New York, ***above***), *Santa Cecilia, Santa Isabel, Santa Luisa, Santa Margarita,* and *Santa Maria*. The other three, the *Santa Clara, Santa Monica,* and *Santa Sofia*, primarily sailed to Caribbean ports, Venezuela, and Colombia. Three-week voyages were priced from $550 in the 1950s, and six-week trips from $975. These ships were air-conditioned, had outdoor pools, and the novelty of an outdoor movie screen that was attached to the aft mast. [Built by North Carolina Shipbuilding Corporation, Wilmington, North Carolina, 1946. 8,357 gross tons; 459 feet long; 63 feet wide. Steam turbines, single screw. Service speed 16 knots. 52 all-first-class passengers.]

∾ PRESIDENT CLEVELAND

While in the early stages of construction, two P2-type troopships were no longer needed by the government after the war ended in August 1945. Their hulls were later sold to American President Lines, who changed the construction and design specifications, and completed the pair in 1947–48 as the *President Cleveland (above)* and *President Wilson*. They made six-week round-trip voyages between San Francisco, Los Angeles, Honolulu, Yokohama, Kobe, Hong Kong, Manila, and then homeward in reverse. The ships were popular both as passenger liners, carrying business and government-related travelers, as well as for cruising, offering complete forty-two-day itineraries. They also carried many Asian immigrants to America in their economy-class quarters. Although no longer used, the economy-class dormitories were still installed when these ships were retired by American President in 1972–73. [Built by Bethlehem-Alameda Shipyard, Alameda, California, 1947. 18,962 gross tons; 609 feet long; 75 feet wide. Steam turbo-electric, twin screw. Service speed 20 knots. 778 passengers (324 first-class, 454 economy-class).]

The first-class quarters on the *President Cleveland* and *President Wilson* were noted for their luxury and comfort. Here we see the First Class Card Room onboard the *Cleveland (opposite, top)*. The room includes leather armchairs, high-gloss linoleum floors, and faces out onto the ship's enclosed promenade area.

The sitting room of an Upper Deck suite on the *President Cleveland (opposite, bottom)* included three large windows overlooking the sea, a large chest of drawers, and twin table lamps with Oriental bases.

∾ EXCAMBION

Four of the very finest American combination liners were the highly popular "Four Aces" of American Export Lines, the *Excalibur*, *Excambion* (seen here, *above*, departing from New York with Brooklyn's Red Hook district in the background), *Exeter*, and *Exochorda*. High standard ships, they featured modern public rooms, a swimming pool on deck, and staterooms that were convertible to living rooms by day. Each cabin also had private bathroom facilities. Notably, the "Aces" were the first fully air-conditioned passenger ships in the world when they first entered commercial service in 1948 (they had actually been built four years before, but as wartime attack transports). In the early 1950s, one of them sailed every other Friday afternoon from New York on forty-two-day round-trips to Cadiz, Barcelona, Marseilles, Naples, Alexandria, Beirut, Naples, Marseilles, Genoa, Leghorn, Barcelona, and back to New York via Boston. The full voyage was priced from $975. Interestingly, the former *Excambion* remains afloat at the time of writing (2002). Used in later years as the maritime cadet training ship *Texas Clipper*, she is mothballed at Beaumont, Texas. [Built by Bethlehem Steel Company, Sparrows Point, Maryland, 1944. 9,644 gross tons; 473 feet long; 66 feet wide. Steam turbines, single screw. Service speed 17 knots. 125 all-first-class passengers.]

∾ CONSTITUTION

With the obvious exception of the *United States*, the two largest and most advanced liners built in the United States after the Second World War were the sisters *Independence* and *Constitution*—seen here arriving at Genoa (*opposite, top*)—of American Export Lines. Completed in January and June 1951, they were the first fully air-conditioned luxury liners ever built. For about fifteen months, the *Independence* also ranked as the fastest ship in the U.S. merchant marine, having reached over 26 knots during her sea trials off the coast of Maine. With amenities including two outdoor pools, these ships were especially designed for the mostly warm-weather mid-Atlantic voyages, sailing between New York, Gibraltar, Naples, Genoa, and Cannes. They, too, were heavily subsidized by the federal government and were said to be

convertible to carry up to 10,000 troops each, should the need arise. Like the *United States* and *America*, these two ships were known for their fine American service, comfortable accommodations, and, especially for their immaculate conditions. [Built by Bethlehem Steel Company, Quincy, Massachusetts, 1951. 29,500 gross tons as built; 683 feet long; 89 feet wide. Steam turbines, twin screw. Service speed 23 knots. 1,000 passengers (295 first-class, 375 cabin-class, 330 tourist-class).]

∾ INDEPENDENCE

The *Independence*, shown here after its 1960 all-white repainting (*opposite, bottom*), and the *Constitution* began to lose transatlantic passengers, and so turned more to one-class cruising. Eventually, American Export lost interest in passenger shipping and retired these ships in the fall of 1968. Idle for six years, they were then sold to Hong Kong-based shipping tycoon C. Y. Tung, who was creating a large passenger fleet of secondhand ships that included the giant former *Queen Elizabeth* and five former American passenger ships, the former *Atlantic*, *Exeter*, and *Excalibur* (all formerly of American Export), and the ex-*President Cleveland* and ex-*President Wilson* (from American President Lines). The two big Export liners were not revived until the early 1980s, however, when, as the renamed *Oceanic Independence* and *Oceanic Constitution*, they were based at Honolulu for Hawaiian island cruise service. They were re-flagged under the American colors and later reverted to their original names. The *Independence* was laid-up in October 2001 when her last owners, American Classic Voyages, closed down in bankruptcy. Her seventeen years in American Export service, combined with her twenty-one years in Hawaiian service, have given her one of the longest careers of all liners under the American flag. The *Constitution*, laid-up in early 1996, sank off Hawaii while empty, under tow, and bound for a Far Eastern scrapyard in November 1997. [*Independence*: Built by Bethlehem Steel Company, Quincy, Massachusetts, 1951. 30,293 gross tons as refitted in 1959; 683 feet long; 89 feet wide. Steam turbines, twin screw. Service speed 23 knots. 1,110 passengers as refitted in 1959 (405 first-class, 375 cabin-class, 330 tourist-class).]

〜 BARRETT

In 1950–1951, American President Lines was building three new combination liners, the *President Jackson*, *President Adams*, and *President Hayes*, for their around-the-world service. But because of the Korean War, the ships were needed instead by the government for trooping and were redesigned as the transports *Barrett (above)*, *Geiger*, and *Upshur*, respectively. Their 204 luxury first-class berths gave way to quarters for 1,896 passengers each. The three ships sailed for MSTS, both in the Atlantic and Pacific, as well as on Caribbean runs to Puerto Rico, Cuba, and the Panama Canal Zone. The *Barrett* went on to make history as the last active U.S.-flag troopship in service when she arrived at Los Angeles on her final voyage in March 1973. [Built by New York Shipbuilding Corporation, Camden, New Jersey, 1951. 13,300 gross tons; 553 feet long; 73 feet wide. Steam turbines, single screw. Service speed 20 knots. 1,896 passengers (396 dependent passengers, 1,500 troops).]

〜 MARIPOSA

In 1956, the Matson Line commissioned two converted Mariner Class freighters, rebuilt as the luxury liners *Mariposa (below)* and *Monterey*, for South Pacific service to Polynesia, New Zealand, and Australia. These ships, with their country-club-like intimacy, became so popular that, on some sailings, more than fifty percent of the passengers were repeaters. In 1970, they transferred to the Pacific Far East Line, another San Francisco-based shipowner, before being retired from U.S.-flag operations altogether in 1978. The *Mariposa* was sold to China in 1983 and sailed for them until scrapped in 1996; the *Monterey* continues under her original name, but for the Italian-based Mediterranean Shipping Cruises. [Built by Bethlehem Steel Corporation, Quincy, Massachusetts, 1953. 14,812 gross tons; 563 feet long; 76 feet wide. Steam turbines, single screw. Service speed 20 knots. 365 all-first-class passengers.]

The dining room aboard the *Mariposa* and *Monterey* had two raised side sections that overlooked the center area *(opposite, top)*.

∾ *ATLANTIC*

Another converted Mariner Class freighter, but with far larger accommodations than the two Matson Line ships, was the *Atlantic* of American Banner Lines *(below)*. She was rebuilt to accommodate as many as 880 passengers in two classes for transatlantic service between New York, Zeebrugge, and Amsterdam. She was commissioned in June 1958, but was completely unsuccessful. As a partnership between the Arnold Bernstein shipping interests and Seafarers' International Union, American Banner lasted but two seasons before, in December 1959, the *Atlantic* was sold to American Export Lines. Keeping her name, she entered New York–Mediterranean service the following May. Refitted for warm-weather sailing, a pool was added to her stern section, an amenity that ranked for a time as the largest of its kind afloat. [Built by Sun Shipbuilding & Dry Dock Company, 1953. 14,138 gross tons; 564 feet long; 76 feet wide. Steam turbines, single screw. Service speed 20 knots. 880 passengers (40 first-class, 840 tourist-class).]

SANTA PAULA

To date, the last luxury liners to be built for American owners were completed in 1958. There was a pair for the Grace Line and a pair for Moore-McCormack. Both companies were heavily involved in the Latin American trades. The Grace sister ships, the *Santa Rosa* and *Santa Paula*, were designed by William Francis Gibbs and, even with their single funnel, had a marked similarity to the far larger *United States*. Along with considerable cargo space, the *Santa Paula*—seen here leaving Newport News Shipyard on her sea trials *(opposite, top)*—had luxurious, all-first-class passenger quarters, which included a good number of suites and deluxe, oversized staterooms. She and her sister ran weekly, thirteen-day, cruiselike voyages from New York to Curacao, La Guaira, Aruba, Kingston, Port au Prince, and Port Everglades in Florida. Fares in the late 1950s began at $595, which was $150–200 above their foreign-flag competitors. [Built by Newport News Shipbuilding & Drydock Company, Newport News, Virginia, 1958. 15,371 gross tons; 584 feet long; 84 feet wide. Steam turbines, twin screw. Service speed 20 knots. 300 all-first-class passengers.]

BRASIL

Moore-McCormack Lines introduced their new *Brasil (opposite, bottom)* in September 1958 and the *Argentina* that December. They were designed for month-long round-trip voyages from New York to Trinidad, Rio de Janeiro, Santos, Montevideo, and Buenos Aires, with an occasional call en route at Port Everglades. Their dummy funnels initially housed a glass-roofed solarium, while exhausts were emitted from the twin uptakes placed farther aft. There were pleasant public rooms, unusually large staterooms, and two swimming pools on deck. Later used more often for cruises to the Caribbean, Eastern Canada, Africa, Europe, and Scandinavia, they actually saw only eleven years of service under U.S. colors. Laid-up in the fall of 1969, they were sold two years later to the Holland America Line, by then using Dutch West Indian registry, and took on new identities. The *Argentina*, which became the *Veendam* for the Dutch, later sailed as the *Monarch Star*, *Brasil* (for a short charter in 1974–75), then back to *Monarch Star*, *Veendam* again, then *Bermuda Star*, *Enchanted Isle*, *Commodore Hotel*, and finally back to *Enchanted Isle*. She was laid-up in late 2000, when her last owners, Commodore Cruise Lines, went bankrupt. The *Brasil* (seen here departing from Boston) became the *Volendam*, *Monarch Sun*, back to *Volendam*, *Island Sun*, *Liberté*, *Canada Star*, *Queen of Bermuda*, *Enchanted Seas*, and finally *Universe Explorer*, the name under which she still sails (as of 2002). [Built by Ingalls Shipbuilding Corporation, Pascagoula, Mississippi, 1958. 23,500 gross tons; 617 feet long; 86 feet wide. Steam turbines, twin screw. Service speed 23 knots. 553 all-first-class passengers.]

SAVANNAH

Beginning in the mid-1950s, the U.S. government saw great potential in employing nuclear power for commercial purposes. The planners in Washington felt that ships were ideal vehicles to display peaceful, practical uses of atomic energy. The prototype was a combination passenger-cargo vessel, with such proposed names as *Atom Queen* and even *Mamie*, after the wife of President Dwight Eisenhower, who saw to the funding for the project. The name *Savannah* was selected as the choice in the end, honoring the first steamship to cross the Atlantic in 1819. Laid down in May 1958, with Vice President Richard Nixon's wife officiating, and then launched in July 1959, with Mrs. Eisenhower presiding over the naming, the $60 million ship *(above)* was ready for her first voyage in August 1962. Initially operated by New York-based States Marine Lines on behalf of the government, the management soon passed on to American Export Lines (renamed American Export–Isbrandtsen Lines in 1962) for demonstration and "open house" voyages to U.S. ports as well as for crossings to Northern Europe and the Mediterranean. But there were many problems, among them the high security at ports, the fear of a fuel leak, and the need for specially trained, higher paid crew members. Furthermore, she was a ship without any comparable partners and therefore did not fit in properly with either American Export's passenger or freight divisions. And so, after the government lost interest in nuclear-powered merchant ships (a fleet of nuclear-powered freighters was actually on the drawing boards as late as 1965–66), Export officials lost interest as well.

By 1972, the *Savannah* was laid-up at its namesake city, but was soon converted to a museum ship at Charleston, South Carolina in 1981. A financial failure, she was repossessed by the Maritime Administration and, sealed tight, was moved to the Federal Reserve Fleet in Virginia's James River. Recently, in 2001, she has been reported to be on the list for scrapping of older, useless tonnage. [Built by the New York Shipbuilding Corporation, Camden, New Jersey, 1958–62. 13,599 gross tons; 595 feet long; 78 feet wide. Nuclear reactor plus steam turbines, twin screw. Service speed 20 knots. 60 all-first-class passengers.]

∾ *Santa* Quartet

Grace Line built the last U.S.-flag, deep-sea passenger ships in 1963–64, a quartet of partially containerized ships for its New York-South American west coast service. They continued the standard of having luxurious, all-one-class accommodations and proved popular with tourists on their twenty-six-day round voyages. Grace eliminated its money-losing passenger division in 1971, however, and within a year, three of the ships were transferred to the Delta Line for passenger sailings from U.S. West Coast on an itinerary completely around South America. The fourth ship, the *Santa Magdalena*, being used as freighter, joined her three sisters in this service by the end of 1974. A decade later, they were retired. While the *Santa Mercedes* went on to become a maritime training ship, the *Patriot State*, the other three were laid-up for a time before going to Taiwanese shipbreakers in 1986. In this view at Alameda, California *(above)*, dated March 9, 1986, we see four of the last remaining passenger ships then still under the U.S. flag: (from left to right) the *Santa Mariana*, the *Monterey*, the *Santa Magdalena* (inboard), nested with the *Santa Maria*. [Built by Bethlehem Steel Company, Sparrows Point, Maryland, 1963. 14,442 gross tons; 547 feet long; 79 feet wide. Steam turbines, single screw. Service speed 20 knots. 119 all-first-class passengers.]

༄

CHAPTER V

SS *United States:*
The Yankee Record-Breaker

"The *United States* was a very special ship," remembered Michael Shernoff, a seasonal crew member aboard her in the late 1960s. "She was the Blue Riband holder, the very fastest liner anywhere in the world. She was not an especially elegant liner, but she was always immaculate, impeccably maintained and provided the very highest level of American service and cuisine at sea." Big, fast, superbly run—these were the qualities that the U.S. government, her benefactors, and United States Lines (her owners and operators) had in mind when planning the ship, just after World War II. William Francis Gibbs, her brilliant designer, always appreciated large liners. He had made plans for many, including a very fast team in the 1920s that would sail from eastern Long Island to Europe, thereby cutting the Atlantic passage time. His work on such ships as Matson Line's 17,200-ton *Malolo* of 1927, the Grace Line's 9,900-ton *Santa Paula* class of 1932, and the 33,900-ton *America* of 1940 were special events, but merely a prelude to his efforts toward what he often referred to as "the big ship"—his ultimate creation.

Serious planning began in 1940, but was delayed due to World War II and its more pressing demands. Planning the "big ship" was relegated to a few Sunday afternoons or summer weekends. But with a turning point in the war, and with probable victory in sight, Gibbs refocused on the project in 1943. By then, the U.S. government was also very keen on large liners that could easily be converted to large-capacity troopships, should another war break out. In particular, the enormous success of the Cunarders *Queen Mary* and *Queen Elizabeth*, each carrying 15,000 soldiers or more per voyage during the war years, was duly noted, especially by the Pentagon. America needed to be ready, and big liners were part of the preparation; as many as eleven liners were said to be considered.

But with the end of the war in the summer of 1945, and a change from a very keen Roosevelt administration to the more conservative Truman period, the American passenger ship project was substantially scaled down. It was finally reduced to one large- and two medium-sized liners and three combination passenger-cargo ships. Possible military use was still an important consideration, but some farsighted government officials also saw airliners as part of the commercial future of transportation, rather than ocean liners. In their opinion, the ocean liner had limited commercial potential. However, airlines would not become a very serious threat for at least another decade, during the second half of the 1950s. Gibbs's "big ship" was still a worthwhile proposition and could look forward to at least a decade of financial return on her commercial sailings. In fact, after her debut in 1952, the *United States* did not begin to lose money until 1962. Thereafter, her government benefactors covered the increasingly high differences between profit and loss.

In all, 145,000 pounds of paper were used in the planning for this, the ultimate ship. These plans were made in the Gibbs & Cox offices in Lower Manhattan, later shipped to the Newport News Shipyard in Virginia, and finally sent over to Washington for final approval by the government. By the late 1940s, the project was a national one, with almost all of the then-forty-eight states contributing something. Press releases became more regular and dutiful newspapers carried fascinating reports, usually just select bits of information, of America's greatest ocean liner. The first photo of a large model of the ship was released in April 1948. There would be subsequent modifications, of course, but the interested public as well as the shipping world now had a clear understanding of what United States Lines was building. She seemed to be the very embodiment of advanced design and sleek proportions—the future. Not yet constructed, she was already said to be the greatest ship of her time.

The first publicly displayed model of the *United States* was presented in April 1948, four years before the ship itself was completed *(opposite, top)*. Details of the top decking would change, the second set of aft king posts would disappear, the radar mast would be simplified, and the two funnels would be slightly redesigned and painted in United States Lines' colors of red, white, and blue. While preliminary designs had started as far back as 1940, with more detailed planning from 1943, the project was said to have actually started on March 26, 1946, when United States Lines proposed the building of a superliner to the federal government, namely the Maritime Commission, with a request for funding.

The plans by Gibbs & Cox for the new ship were approved on April 5, 1948. Funding was given congressional approval that summer. Construction bids were submitted that August: $67,350,000 from the Newport News Shipbuilding & Dry Dock Company, the builders of the *America*, and $75,649,000 from Bethlehem Steel Company's Quincy, Massachusetts plant. Subsequent amendments put the actual cost of the new ship at $70,373,000. A purely commercial ship of the same size would have cost $43 million, but the wartime defense features required by the government increased by the total cost by about $27 million. In the end, United States Lines paid approximately $28 million of the total cost, with the government responsible for the additional $42 million. Newport News ultimately won the contract to build the ship, and the final papers were signed on May 3, 1949. This view *(opposite, bottom)*, dated February 8, 1950, shows the official keel laying.

The great bow section is seen in this photo *(above)*, also from February 8, 1950. The initial design for the ship was presented in 400 different plans, sketches, and diagrams to the Newport News Shipyard, which were then translated into about 4,600 detailed working plans. By this time, the naming of the ship had been resolved. Initial ideas included such names as *Columbia, Hudson, Mayflower, New York*, or even *American Engineer*. In the adjacent slipway at Newport News, construction had begun on a new aircraft carrier, the USS *United States*. However, the Navy soon canceled that project and the name "United States" became available. It seemed the ideal choice to the directors of United States Lines.

The total hours of technical work, investigation, and research applied by both Gibbs & Cox and the Newport News Shipyard were greater than any other marine project to date. Later, in 1952, William Francis Gibbs denied that he was the sole designer of this great ship. "About fifty percent of the maritime engineering brains of the country have been applied to this vessel," he said. "A great ship is the most complicated structure a man creates. Top-flight American manufacturers produced important refinements in design especially for her. This ship is the product of a prodigious power: American industry." Clearly, America had never built such a large and advanced vessel, commercial or otherwise. She would be an epoch-making ship in many ways, but especially in its value for national defense, safety, and speed. Newport News was, however, planning large aircraft carriers that would surpass the *United*

States in size. Here *(opposite, top)* we see the liner's stern section in the first phases of assembly. Two of the shaft lines are visible.

For security reasons, the *United States* was created in a large graving dock rather than the traditional building slip at Newport News *(opposite, bottom)*. Muscular cranes worked from platforms high above the actual construction base.

Within six months, by the winter of 1950, almost fifty percent of the overall structure of the ship was in place *(above)*. She was constructed in Slipway No. 10 at Newport News, which was actually 960 feet long (as well as 123 feet wide and 35 feet below sea level). With an excess of 30 feet, the ship's overall length of 990 feet projected both at the bow and the stern over the inboard and the outboard ends of the slipway.

Gibbs took the funnel design of the *America* and, with refinements and increases in size, devised similar ones for the *United States*. In this scene staged for publicity (*opposite, top*), ten standard American automobiles are used to show the width of the liner's second, all-aluminum funnel.

The aft funnel was fitted on May 23, 1951 (*opposite, bottom*). The two funnels, sixty feet long and fifty-five feet high, had been sub-assembled of aluminum and had to be erected in two pieces for crane clearance reasons.

Within days, the funnels were painted in United States Lines' color scheme of a blue top, white band, and red bottom (*above*). The Boat Deck area is still bare and open since the davits and lifeboats have not yet been fitted.

In the final days before the ship is officially named and floated out, cranes hover over the ship like bridal attendants before a wedding *(above)*. The dock area will be flooded over a period of just under fifty-four hours so that, exactly 500 days from the keel laying, the *United States* would be launched. Note also how those mighty funnels, her most visible components, already dominate the ship. Gibbs greatly admired very large funnels and how they suggested a ship's size, power, and speed. The *United States* was located at Hull No. 488 at Newport News.

The *United States* is seen in this stern view on the morning of her naming, June 23, 1951 *(opposite, top)*. An official at the Newport News Shipyard proudly observed, "Already, in outward appearance, the *United States* somewhat resembles a huge yacht with her raking bow, cruiser stern, and unbroken promenade deck line from the bow to within a few feet of the extreme stern. The trim appearance is accentuated by the two large, streamlined, and well-raked stacks."

First Lady Bess Truman had been asked to name the new liner, but was pressed to decline. At the time, there was a debate in Congress over the decision to send the new liner into troopship service for the Korean War being fought in the Pacific. President Truman was said to be concerned about the debate, and wanting to avoid taking sides, insisted that Mrs. Truman politely refuse the offer. Instead, the wife of Texas senator Tom Connally was selected to do the honors. She is seen here *(opposite, bottom)*, in a photo dated June 13, 1951, ten days before the actual ceremonies. With a model of the ship before them (clearly, an original creation with the added aft king posts that were never used), Senator Connally is to the right of his wife. On the far left is an official from United States Lines, and to the far right, a representative from the Maritime Commission.

Saturday, June 23, 1951: the great day arrived (*opposite*). Dignitaries, including Mrs. Connally, are assembled on the mounted platform for speeches, dedications, and the naming of the ship. Great, billowing bunting has been affixed to the top of the sleek, razorlike bow.

The christening wine splashes as the name *United States* is officially given to the ship (*above*). Several thousand officials, workers, and their families witnessed the special event.

With the graving dock opened and flooded, a small armada of tugs assists the liner as she moves out of the slip (*left*). The American flag flies from the stern for the first time.

The great ship is now cleared of the slipway as no less than eight tugs carefully begin to shift her to the right, headed for the fitting-out berth *(opposite, top)*.

The *United States* was built of steel and aluminum *(opposite, bottom)*. The main portion of the hull, up to and including the Promenade Deck is steel; above the Promenade Deck, the super-structure is mainly aluminum. Steel was used for the house front and all structure forward, while the major part of the aluminum, riveted with aluminum welding, was used only where strength was not required. Special attention was given to the design of the stern structure in order to minimize hull vibration. As a result, specially

constructed bulkheads, girders, and brackets were installed. The bow section is formed of various radius plating from the upper end to the waterline. The use of over 2,000 tons of aluminum consti-tuted the largest single order of that material yet placed.

Armies of workers leave the *United States* during lunch hour on November 14, 1951 *(above)*. Their task was massive but highly organized. Together, they created a moving hotel—a floating city. Items fitted to the magnificent ship included 125,000 pieces of china, 6,000 crystal goblets, 7,000 bedspreads, 4,000 passenger blankets, 44,000 bed sheets, 81,000 face towels, and 7 caskets for the hospital.

With smoke billowing from the forward funnel (*opposite, top*), dock trials for the new liner were held for three days, beginning on March 26, 1952. "She was satisfactory in all respects," was the comment from the builders. The U.S. Coast Guard added to the excitement and anticipation of her completion in three months' time when it stated, "Americans are building a ship which will give this country [the] best representation on the sea lanes of the world it has had since the days of the clipper. Excelling in many respects over other ships of the world, it will have safety features which will make it the safest passenger or troopship in operation anywhere. One of the great features of the steamship *United States* is the improvement in fire safety. This is due largely to the elimination of combustible materials. All wood trim and veneers have been eliminated, and all draperies, upholstery, and mattresses will receive fire-retardant treatment. Every article of furniture must be constructed of fire-retardant materials. Where passageways pierce fire bulkheads, automatic fire doors are installed. All can be closed simultaneously from the bridge. In addition to the latest navigating instruments, the subdivision of the hull is unprecedented for a merchant ship. A flick of a switch will close all power-operated, watertight doors. Even the lifeboats on the ship will be constructed entirely without wood. The *United States* will carry 2,000 passengers under conditions of unexcelled comfort and safety."

The *United States* had two sets of sea trials, all held approximately 100–150 miles off the Virginia Capes in the North Atlantic. Earlier plans for time-consuming trial runs off Rockland, Maine or down to Guantanamo, Cuba were dropped. Officials and crews from the Newport News Shipyard manned the ship during the trials, which were longer and more exacting than usual because of its size, innovation, and highly secret propulsion and speed capabilities. The ship, outbound for the first time on May 14, 1952, is headed for a three-day trial voyage (*opposite, bottom*). A United States Lines' freighter, the *American Harvester*, is on the port side, inbound at Hampton Roads.

While largely top secret at the time, the trials of the *United States* were a blazing success. At the time, it was publicly revealed that she had 158,000 shaft horsepower—slightly more than Cunard's *Queen Mary*, then the world's fastest liner—giving the American flagship a top speed of approximately 30 knots. There had been rumors that the Americans had previously made a secret pact with the British not to break the *Queen Mary*'s record. Another rumor circulated that the *Queen Elizabeth* might have a try at the Blue Riband, given to the ship with the fastest transatlantic crossing, but then Cunard would actually be beating itself. In reality, the *Queen Mary*'s record from 1938 had already been surpassed by the Navy aircraft carrier *Lake Champlain*, which crossed from Norfolk to Gibraltar in 4 days, 8 hours, and 51 minutes at an average speed of just over 32 knots in the fall of 1945. But as a military ship, she was not eligible for the Blue Riband. After the *United States* was officially declassified by the Navy Department in 1968, it was finally revealed that she made an exceptional 43 knots during a phase of the trials, and even did 20 knots in reverse as seen in this rare photograph (*above*). In actuality, she was the most powerful liner ever built, with over 241,000 horsepower.

At two o'clock in the afternoon of Tuesday, June 10, 1952, the *United States* began to reduce speed at the end of her second set of trials *(right)*. At approximately seven-thirty that evening, her trial records noted, "All secure fore and aft to shipyard pier, gangways aboard." Following some final adjustments and outfitting, the great ship was ready to be delivered to United States Lines, seven weeks in advance of the contracted delivery date.

The liner was formally handed over to United States Lines on June 22, 1952 (*above*). William Francis Gibbs is seated second from the left.

Over 1,200 company officials, special guests, and a large number of reporters and photographers joined the short, overnight voyage northward from Newport News to New York. Seen here while in the Lower Bay off Staten Island (*below*), the *United States* is dressed in flags and escorted by a growing fleet of tugs, cutters, spectator boats and pleasure craft as she arrives to a thunderous horn-blowing and whistle-sounding reception on June 23, 1952.

Two Liberty ships and a Staten Island commuter ferryboat are to the port side as the *United States* majestically makes her way along the Upper Bay, toward the mouth of the Hudson River (*opposite, top*). Ellis Island is to the far left, a tip of Governor's Island to the right.

"The harbor was not silent for a moment," remembered Frank Braynard, then a maritime reporter who was aboard the *United States* at the time. "Everything that could make a sound did so to welcome this new beauty, the greatest ship ever built by America." A party was held at the United Fruit Company pier at Rector Street in Lower Manhattan (*opposite, bottom*). Just behind, large banners are proudly displayed at the building at 21 West Street, which contained the offices of Gibbs & Cox.

There was a great open house for several days as visitors, prospective passengers, and yet more reporters and travel writers went aboard the new liner at Pier 86 (*left*). At noon on Wednesday, July 3, 1952, she departed on her first voyage to Europe. It was expected to be a record run and, fortunately, the weather and sea conditions cooperated.

73

William Francis Gibbs and Margaret Truman, the daughter of President Harry Truman, were among the passengers on the first crossing (*above*). Commodore Harry Manning was in command. Fares for the inaugural trip started at $360 in first-class, $230 in cabin-class, and $170 in tourist-class. Some of the ship's basic statistics were revealed to the press at this time, including the final price tag, which was put at approximately $72 million. The total passengers and crew was placed at 3,101 and, in an emergency, her troop capacity was said to be 12–14,000 (it could have exceeded 15,000 if needed). [Built by Newport News Shipbuilding & Dry Dock Company, Newport News, Virginia, 1952. 53,329 gross tons; 990 feet long; 101 feet wide. Steam turbines, quadruple screw. Service speed 28–30 knots. 2,008 passengers (913 first-class, 558 cabin-class, 537 tourist-class).]

The maiden crossing was an enormous success. En route, she passed the westbound French liner *Liberté*, herself a former Blue Riband champion from the early 1930s in her first career as Germany's *Europa*. She reported to the French Line's Paris headquarters that the new American flagship was "making an incredible speed in excess of 35 knots!" Seen here (*opposite, top*) speed-

ing across the English Channel bound for Le Havre, her first port of call, on July 7, the *United States* shaved 10 hours and 2 minutes off the *Queen Mary*'s best record, made in 1938. The American superliner's eastbound record was 3 days, 10 hours, and 40 minutes, an astounding average of 35.59 knots, on the traditional routing between New York's Ambrose Light House and Bishop's Rock in Cornwall, England. The *Queen Mary*'s average back in 1938 was 3.9 knots less. Next, the *United States* would try for the westbound record. It had been exactly one hundred years since another American passenger vessel, the *Baltic* of the Collins Line, had captured the Riband. Her record crossing was 9 days and 13 hours, at an average speed of 13.34 knots.

The British gave the *United States* the most enthusiastic welcome since the *Queen Mary*'s maiden voyage in June 1936. Winston Churchill sent a congratulatory telegram, as did other government officials and the directors of rival Cunard. Twenty thousand people welcomed the new Yankee speed champion as she berthed at the Ocean Terminal in Southampton on July 8 (*opposite, bottom*).

The westbound maiden voyage was another success: 3 days, 12 hours, and 12 minutes. This time, the average speed was posted at 34.51 knots. President Truman traveled to New York and welcomed the liner upon her return to Pier 86. Milton Berle and Margaret Truman were among the returning passengers. The *United States* became the most famous ocean liner in the world, subsequently carrying more passengers than any other single liner on the North Atlantic, and settling down to a very popular rotation of crossings between New York, Le Havre, Southampton, and Bremerhaven. Here we see her at Southampton's Western Docks on October 3, 1960 (*opposite*). The American aircraft carrier USS *Antietam* is at dock, and two Union-Castle Line passenger ships are just behind—the laid-up, scrap-yard-bound *Carnarvon Castle* and the brand-new *Windsor Castle*.

At Le Havre, the *United States* is seen departing (*top*) as three French Line passenger ships are docked in the background of this 1952 view: the *Liberté* to the left and, on the far right, the *Ile de France* and the *Antilles*.

Once during a dockers' strike at Le Havre, the *United States* was detoured to Cherbourg, where she is seen in this dramatic nighttime view (*middle*).

The *United States* became very popular with German passengers, especially since Germany's transatlantic liners were under Allied restriction and did not resume service until 1955, ten years after the end of the Second World War. Like United States Lines' passenger ships in the 1920s and '30s, the *United States* even carried some crew of German-born, naturalized American citizens. They mainly worked in the passenger departments as waiters, stewards, and kitchen help. On these extended Atlantic voyages, Bremerhaven would be the European turn-around port, usually requiring an overnight stay. The *United States* is seen here (*bottom*) at that port's Columbus Quay.

The *United States* almost always returned to New York very early in the morning, docking before eight o'clock and then disembarking her passengers at ten. She remained in port for three or four days. In this splendid aerial view (*overleaf*), she is just entering the slip between Piers 86 and 88 along Manhattan's West Side. American Export Lines' *Independence* is already berthed at adjacent Pier 84 while, to the right, Italian Line's *Cristoforo Colombo* and, farther downstream, Cunard's *Queen Mary* are still in midstream.

SS UNITED STATES: THE YANKEE RECORD-BREAKER / 77

Sometimes as many as six Moran tugboats were required to assist with the docking and undocking of such large liners (*above*). Because of her very large and wide funnels, wind was always a special consideration with the *United States*. During tugboat strikes, she had to carefully dock herself, a slow process that took as much as triple the normal time.

On one occasion, in 1953, the *United States* made a deliberate midday arrival so that she could pass the outbound *America*, which had left Pier 86 at noon. This well-known photograph (*opposite, top*) created an interesting comparison between the two greatest U.S.-flag ocean liners of their time.

On February 18, 1958, the otherwise impeccable record of arrivals and departures for the *United States* was disrupted for a few hours by both bitterly cold weather and an ice-choked Hudson River (*opposite, bottom*). Tugs gently assist the liner as she heads for the north side of Pier 86.

Very often, the *United States* was caught in the great groupings of Atlantic liners at New York's appropriately named "Luxury Liner Row." Photos of these occasions often appeared in the following day's newspapers. In this scene *(opposite, top)*, dated August 20, 1952, five luxury ships are in port, which from top to bottom, are the *America*, the *United States*; the *Ile de France*, French Line; and the *Georgic* and *Queen Elizabeth*, Cunard Line.

In this 1958 view *(opposite, bottom)*, from top to bottom, there are the *Olympia*, Greek Line; the *United States* and *America*; and American Export's *Independence*.

At the end of each transatlantic season, usually by November, the *United States* returned to her birthplace, the Newport News Shipyards, for her annual overhaul, special repairs, and major housecleaning. The mighty bow section is seen here *(above)* with painters' scaffolds hung along her sides.

Those fifty-five-foot-high funnels were groomed each year as well (*opposite, top*).

Photos of the highly secret underwater hull form (*opposite, bottom*) were permissible only after the ship was declassified in 1968.

A comparison of great size (*above*): the *United States* is being repaired and overhauled in Dock No. 10 at Newport News Shipyard, the same slip in which she was built, while the giant, nuclear-powered aircraft carrier USS *Enterprise* is to the left. This view dates from November 1964.

SS UNITED STATES: THE YANKEE RECORD-BREAKER / 85

The *United States* was overhauled within New York harbor on only three rare occasions. The liner was placed in the large graving dock at the Naval Annex, located off the Lower Bay in Bayonne, New Jersey. In this instance (*above*) on July 21, 1954, hurriedly scheduled between crossings, she will have her bottom scraped, some quick repainting, and adjustments made to her propellers. Afterward, it is back to regular service.

CHAPTER VI

Making Waves: The World's Fastest Ocean Liner

"While I was only a part-time crew member onboard the *United States* in the late 1960s, I felt enormously proud of her and how she represented our country on the North Atlantic," remembered Michael Shernoff, who worked as a restaurant waiter. "We were competing then against the superliners of the British [namely the *Queen Mary* and *Queen Elizabeth*, and later the *Queen Elizabeth 2*], the French [the *France*], and the Italians [the *Michelangelo* and *Raffaello*]. The *United States* was the mighty symbol of American ingenuity, style, and technology. Especially seeing those great funnels lit up at night at Bremerhaven, Southampton, or Le Havre always elicited a huge surge of patriotic pride in so far as this was the ultimate symbol of America's peacetime might and power."

Architect Robert Allan, also a keen ocean liner enthusiast, added, "She was the most dramatic ocean liner I had ever seen. Her proportions were just perfect with those two silo-sized funnels, which were as wide as they were tall, and that long, very low hull. The *United States* was a ship of perfect planning, perfect order." Ocean liner preservationist Tom Chirby added, "The *United States* was pure maritime thoroughbred. She was the very essence of hydro-dynamic efficiency. She was ocean liner design at its very peak. She was the fitting end to a great era, to a long line of transatlantic behemoths."

In the early years, there was always some speculation that the *United States* would break her own speed records. "This was nonsense," said a former ship's officer. "It would have been foolish, as well as very costly, to do that. What would it have achieved?" Her great popularity was also bonded to the times, the 1950s. America was seen as the great victor of the Second World War, the master industrialist of the postwar era and, of course, the dominant power in the West. On the seas, the *United States* symbolized the national superiority. She was the fastest, most advanced, safest and, in ways, most modern liner of her time. "She was clean, smart, and simple. And she was like Americans—she wasn't stuffy," noted her former Chief Purser David Fitzgerald. "She was much more friendly than, say, the big 'Cunarders' of that period. There was more conversation—friendly conversation—between the passengers and the staff. She was generally a happy-working ship and this high spirit pervaded throughout. She also had superb physical layout, which made her an easy ship in which to get about. First- and cabin-class were extremely well run. She was also meticulous, shining from end to end, and to the very end of her days. We drew lots of American passengers not only from a patriotic sense, but because they felt that they would be better understood on a U.S.-flag ship. We also got many Europeans because they wanted to experience the American style and manners. We carried many, many loyalist passengers—guests who went to Europe every June and then returned to New York in late August or September. "

Not surprisingly, William Francis Gibbs adored the ship that he largely created. Until his death in 1967, he monitored her every arrival and departure. When she was inbound, Gibbs would routinely be driven by his chauffeur to Shore Parkway in Brooklyn to observe the ship, even in pre-dawn darkness, as she passed through the Narrows and, in later years, under the Verrazano Narrows Bridge. The car then raced northward to Pier 86, where Gibbs would watch the docking procedures. He was among the first to go aboard and usually went directly to the captain's quarters and then to the chief engineer's quarters to assess her performance. During his observations, he was reputed to have never used a notebook, due to his exceptional ability to retain details. On outbound sailing days, Gibbs visited the liner before her midday departures and then, in his car, sped down the West Side Highway and watched the ship sail past his Lower Manhattan office windows. Rightfully, he was very proud of one of the finest liners to ever sail the seas.

As the flagship of the entire American merchant marine, and especially as the world's fastest liner, the *United States* enjoyed great recognition, enormous popularity, and tremendous appeal to travelers, regulars, and first-timers alike. A maiden-season company advertisement touted some of her praiseworthy traits: "Less than 5 days to Europe . . . nearly 1,000 feet in length . . . twelve decks in height . . . air conditioned throughout—temperature controlled individually in each stateroom . . . twenty-four public rooms, two theaters . . . swimming pools and gymnasium . . . nineteen elevators . . . staterooms larger than you'd think possible . . . telephones in every stateroom . . . three fine American orchestras . . . electronic, radar ranges cook delicious food in seconds . . . American and international cuisine." Here (*above*), with some painting being done to the tip of her razor-sharp bow, the *United States* waits at New York's Pier 86 between crossings.

The *United States* loaded and offloaded cargo during her stays in New York. Here we see a Ford sedan being loaded aboard in 1957 (*opposite, top*). She has four exposed hatches on the Promenade Deck: two forward (for stores, general cargo, and automobiles) and two aft (the third for baggage, the fourth for mail). There was actually a fifth hold, located adjacent to the second, and used for additional baggage and stores. Provisioning the ship at the beginning of each crossing meant an extensive shopping list that included 16 tons of fresh vegetables, 29½ tons of meat, 3 tons of ice cream, 15 tons of beer, and a ton of ice cubes.

Through much of her career, the *United States* sailed from New York at noon. Reportedly, she was late only once. Great excitement and anticipation prevailed with each departure (*opposite, bottom*), with passengers and visitors arriving at Pier 86 as early as eight o'clock in the morning.

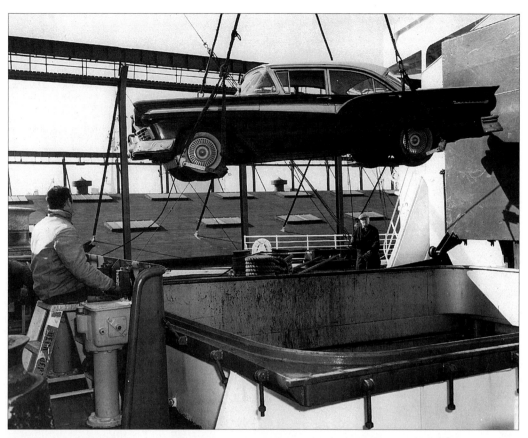

In the early years, a band played music as passengers boarded the *United States*. This view *(above)* dates from her second sailing to Europe, July 15, 1952.

There were separate gangways for each class—first, cabin, and tourist—as well as for visitors and crew *(left)*. Note the special flat wooden bumpers that separated the liner from the pilings of the pier.

Onboard, there were bon voyage parties, unpacking, special details to be handled at the purser's office, and possibly a last-minute change in dining room arrangements. At eleven-thirty, a full half-hour before sailing, the thunderous whistles signaled "all ashore that's going ashore." Visitors filed back onto the dock, and some went to the waterside end of the pier to bid their very final farewells *(opposite, top)*. Many indelible memories were formed as huge, gleaming liners such as the *United States* sailed past and out into the Hudson, beginning a voyage across the Atlantic Ocean. Family and friends might not be seen for months.

A few visitors preferred to see the liners off from the street side of the pier *(opposite, bottom)*, from Twelfth Avenue and just below the West Side Highway.

In this instance *(above)*, two American liners both sail at noon: American Export Lines' *Constitution* (left) bound for Algeciras, Naples, Genoa, and Cannes, and the *United States* (right) headed to Le Havre, Southampton, and Bremerhaven. The stern section of the *America* can be seen on the far right.

Outbound along the lower Hudson in this 1960 view *(opposite, top)*, the *United States* passes tugs with barges in tow, commuting ferries, and, in this case, the inbound Norwegian freighter *Lista*. The Woolworth Building is to the left of the other towers of the Lower Manhattan skyline. Two years later, on July 1, 1962, the *United States* reached her tenth anniversary. She had made 452 crossings by then, carried 653,638 passengers at an average of 88.5% capacity, and cost $20 million a year to operate, a third of which went to crew wages. By then, she had clocked 1,605,000 miles.

Another fine view *(opposite, bottom)*: the *United States* steams in the Upper Bay, passing Governor's Island and headed for the Narrows and then the open Atlantic. To New York harbor observers, she was well known and often highly praised. "She had a perfect hull and superstructure," according to designer and ocean liner collector Mario Pulice. "The balance of her long, sleek hull, knife-edged bow, low superstructure, and all capped by those incredible, massive, tear-shaped stacks was truly a great sight. I was always struck by her stature. She was always a very proud ship when underway. She even looks fast when she is tied-up at the dock. I was always impressed by the great balance of her exterior."

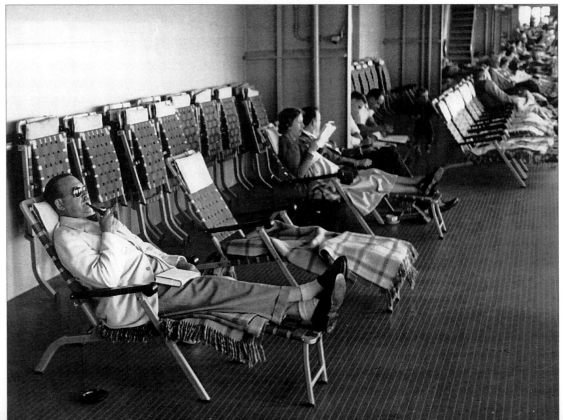

At sea, according to a frequent passenger, "the *United States* had a tremendous sense of speed, urgency, purpose." Her designers, builders, and owners were rightfully proud that she was rarely delayed by harsh weather, but had the capability of making up time if needed *(opposite, top)*. Once, during a cruise sailing, she was delayed by high winds. Later, she sailed as fast as an incredible 40 knots to make up lost time and reach her next port of call on schedule.

Transoceanic travelers often found the enclosed Promenade Deck *(opposite, bottom)* a refuge from the outdoor decks and the often-uncomfortable North Atlantic weather.

Alternately, summer crossings with warmer weather often meant a great demand for deck chairs on the top decks *(above)*. "The green sea and blue sky make a perfect setting for sun lovers," noted a United States Lines brochure.

Those big funnels made an impressive sight from the ship's top decks when at sea *(right)*. The wind often howled as the ship made headway at well over 30 knots.

Within, the *United States* may not have been very luxurious nor elegant, especially when compared to other big Atlantic liners, but instead was quite simple, understated, almost functional. The traditional woods used in ships for decades were, of course, not used because of the great emphasis on fire-retardant materials. Nothing flammable could be used. This posed problems for the decorators, Dorothy Marckwald and Anne Uruquart, the only firm of women ship decorators in the world in the early 1950s. Simplicity was the tone and the decorative theme was an appropriate reflection of American life, using the country's natural elements—the Mississippi River, Navajo Indian sand painting, old American glassware, coastal marine plants and creatures, American industry, and even American philosophy. Natural elements such as the wind, sea, and stars did prevail, however, such that a wide range of greens and blues were used throughout the ship. The first-class ballroom shown here (*opposite, top*) extended the full width of the ship and had a dual purpose: cocktail bar at one end, lounge area at the other. The main decorative feature was the nineteen carved glass panels portraying sea themes. The floor was covered in dark red carpeting (removable for dancing), off-white curtains draped the windows and some bulkheads, and chairs done in a bright coral weave were placed around pedestal-style aluminum tables. In the cocktail portion of this room, the banquettes were done in dark red leather. A grand piano was installed, as well as a wall clock in a celestial motif. A Meyer Davis orchestra played as the featured entertainment in this room.

The First-Class Observation Lounge (*opposite, bottom*) was far forward and designed in the general shape of the letter "H." There was a writing room on the port side and a library on the starboard. The walls were done in a light blue-gray shade known as "mist," the carpeting in bright green, and the chairs and sofas in matching tones. Three types of tables were used: large circular, small circular, and others for card playing. Altogether, there was 15,500 pieces of furniture onboard the *United States*. In this room, a small altar for church services was tucked behind folding doors.

The First-Class Dining Room (*above*) could seat 390 persons at one sitting. The flooring was done in black linoleum and the walls in oyster white. The two-deck-high center portion of the ship was framed in aluminum and gold, and had a musicians' balcony at one end.

Fine crested crystal and crockery, along with hand-polished silver, created attractive table settings in the three restaurants on the *United States* (*below*).

The First-Class Grill Room was an auxiliary restaurant that sat fifty passengers (*above*). The floor and walls were dark blue with the ceiling painted in light gray. The banquettes were sapphire blue and the chairs were either red or gray-white. On the walls, four blue-painted panels contained illuminated crystals in formations based on the stars and planets.

The First-Class Library (*opposite, top*) was a part of the Observation Lounge. A soothing, restful space, it had sea green carpeting and light blue walls.

There were 695 suites and staterooms aboard the *United States*. All of those in first- and cabin-class had private bathroom facilities, while those in tourist-class used public baths and toilets. In all rooms, regardless of class, the furniture was custom-made, with the bedspreads, curtains, and chair upholsteries made from fire-resistant materials. There were fourteen master suites: six on the

Upper Deck and eight on the Main Deck. The furnishings and fabrics used in these were of the highest quality and not used anywhere else on the ship. These three-room suites, said to be the most spacious afloat in the 1950s, consisted of two bedrooms, a sitting room, three bathrooms, a dressing room, and a trunk room. They were priced at $1,200 per person for the five-day crossings in the early 1960s. Each suite had a different decorative theme. U-89, the so-called "Duck Suite," preferred by the Duke and Duchess of Windsor for their twice-a-year voyages, had a center sitting room with walls covered in aluminum leaf depicting ducks in a natural setting (*opposite, bottom*). The carpets were gray, the furniture in lighter gray, and the hand-loomed curtains were off-white. There were four chairs, two in soft gray and two in orange. The colors of other suites ranged from pale sepia to Venetian red, with decorative touches such as seashells and native American trees.

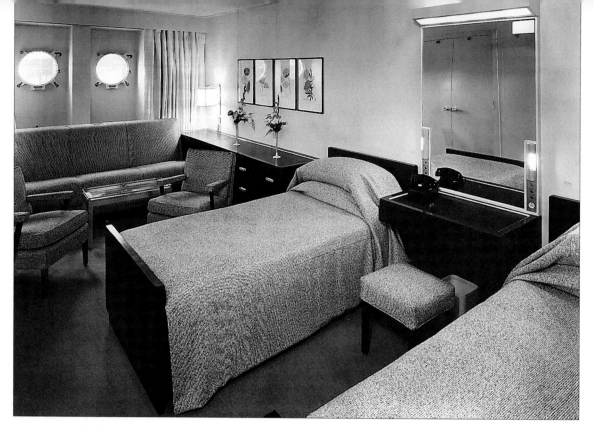

The bedrooms of the top suites aboard the *United States* were very spacious in their own right (***above***). Extra-large wardrobes, dressing tables, and dressers were part of the arrangement.

Six different color schemes were used in decorating the first-class cabins. The walls were done in beige, light blue, gray, light terracotta, and oyster white with either dark blue or dark green furniture. Six different colors were also used in the cabin- and tourist-class rooms. In this Cabin-Class Main Deck stateroom (***below***), the bedspreads and matching draperies have a butterfly theme overlaid on grays and whites, with carpeting in red loop pile.

The Cabin-Class Smoking Room (***opposite, top***) was square in shape and included black leather chairs, black marbleized flooring, putty-colored walls, and a mural behind the bar depicting historic American bottles and jugs. The banquettes along the sides of the room were in beige leather, and the glass-topped tables and mounted ashtrays were made from aluminum.

The Cabin-Class Dining Room, done in midnight blue, extended the full width of the ship (***opposite, bottom***). There were aluminum line sculptures on the walls depicting the four seasons in a constellation motif, gray flooring, and bright green leather chairs.

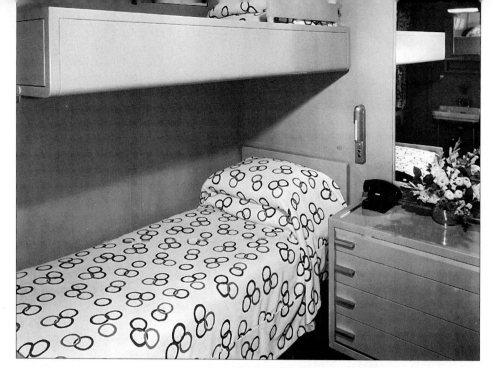

Tourist-class cabins were decorated in three color schemes: light terra-cotta, gray-green, and dark green. In this inside double *(opposite, top)*, there was red leather upholstery and Dynel bedspreads in a loop design.

The Tourist-Class Main Lounge *(opposite, middle)* consisted of chairs done in blue-green or beige, four framed water colors, and Venetian blinds to cover the portholes.

The Tourist-Class Theater *(opposite, bottom)* could seat 200 and was located aft on the Promenade Deck. The stage curtain had bright green geometrical designs, and the seating was done in gun-metal gray.

Like all passenger ships, the quarters for the staff—officers and crew alike—was less elaborate. This officer's day room-office with adjoining bedroom *(above)* had linoleum flooring and leather chairs.

This crew lounge aboard the *United States* included sofas, magazine tables, and writing desks *(below)*.

First-class passenger manifests aboard the *United States* almost always included celebrities and recognizable names. In her first decade of operation, there were voyagers such as Bob Hope, Rita Hayworth, Joan Crawford, Mary Pickford, Cary Grant, John Wayne, Spencer Tracy, Katharine Hepburn, Marilyn Monroe, Greer Garson, Kim Novak, Jackie Gleason, Victor Mature, Charlton Heston, Rex Harrison, Jack Benny, Maurice Chevalier, Marlon Brando, Van Johnson, Jane Wyman, Walt Disney, Leonard Bernstein, Irving Berlin, and Mahalia Jackson. Other notable passengers included Eleanor Roosevelt, Mr. and Mrs. John F. Kennedy, former Presidents Truman and Eisenhower and their wives, the Emperor of Ethiopia, the President of Liberia, Salvador Dalí, Anne and Charlotte Ford, J. Paul Getty, and New York's Francis Cardinal Spellman.

The most famous and well-publicized of the ship's passengers, however, were perhaps the Duke and Duchess of Windsor, seen here *(top, left)* meeting reporters in the Observation Lounge before sailing for Le Havre and then onward to their residence in Paris. Beginning in 1952, the Windsors made two sets of crossings per year on the American flagship, usually once in February and again in June. In winter, they were en route through New York to or from Palm Beach, Florida. "United States Lines was very, very proud to have the former king of England as a regular passenger," said Raymond Kane, a Smoking Room steward aboard the *United States* in early 1950s. "They were treated like royalty. There were no rules for them. Even their pug dogs were allowed to stay with them and not banished to the kennels. It was a priceless testimonial to the company and to the *United States*. They were the ultimate celebrity passengers back then."

Other royal passengers included Queen Frederica of Greece and, on the left, her daughter Princess Irene *(bottom, left)*. The small child in a Greek costume was part of the welcoming delegation for the Queen's arrival at New York in 1958.

Hollywood royalty included film queen Greta Garbo, seen here disembarking at Pier 86 in 1955 *(opposite, top)*.

Actor James Stewart and his family were also passengers aboard the *United States* in the 1950s *(opposite, bottom)*.

By the early 1960s, however, the transatlantic liner trade was in decline. There were fewer passengers, even in the normally peak summer months. In winter, as an alternative, the *United States* was temporarily restyled as a one-class ship, but using only first- and cabin-class accommodations, and sent on more profitable cruises to Bermuda, the Bahamas, and the Caribbean. There were more activities onboard to cater to these new and different passengers—sun-seeking tourists. A portable pool was placed on the outer decks, more daytime games were organized, and the daily activities included golf clinics (*opposite, top*).

From 1962 through 1969, the *United States* was seen on occasion at such tropic, warm-weather ports as San Juan, St. Thomas, Kingston, Cristobal, and Curacao, as shown here (*opposite, bottom*). Also, she began to make some longer cruises, calling at the likes of Rio de Janeiro, Dakar, Capetown, Lisbon, and Gibraltar.

Seen here in 1969 during a cruise call at St. Thomas (*above*), the seventeen-year-old *United States* was scheduled for her longest cruise itinerary yet—a fifty-five-day trip around the Pacific (including Australia, Hong Kong, Japan, and Hawaii) in early 1970. But soon after she reached the Newport News Shipyard in November 1969 for her annual overhaul, her sailing days ended abruptly. Like several Atlantic shipowners, United States Lines decided to pull out of the struggling passenger trade, canceling all future voyages, including another round of crossings set for the next year. Having lost money for years and no longer considered useful by the government in case of war, the once-great pride of the entire American merchant marine was laid-up. Her much-needed subsidy monies were reallocated to the company's still-bustling freighter business. By 1969, the *United States* was losing close to $5 million a year, and the federal government was subsidizing as much as $400 for every passenger carried. The high costs of a U.S.-flag operation made the liner business an expensive venture, especially due to the long, costly strikes among industry workers. It had all become rather hopeless. Moore-McCormack Lines ended their passenger liner services two months before, in September 1969, and the Matson Line pulled out by the summer of 1970. Both American President and Grace lines would follow a short time afterward.

CHAPTER VII

Decay and Decline: Decades in Limbo

As this book was being prepared, the once-immaculate *United States* has spent the last thirty-three years in lay-up condition: unlit, stripped, rusting, decaying, even listing slightly. The sight has been painful for many. "Her long neglect is a national disgrace," stated Michael Shernoff, a former crew member. "I think that she deserves to be back in New York, to be moored along the Hudson, perhaps opposite the Javits Convention Center at West 39th Street. She would be an ideal annex to the Center [as] a hotel and possibly a museum about ocean liners and the history of the Port of New York. Herself, she is great history. She needs to be enshrined along the Manhattan waterfront where she once reigned supreme as the queen of the American passenger fleet."

The *United States* had been unexpectedly yanked from service in November 1969, her seventeenth year of service. She had become too expensive to operate and lacked passengers — in short, a white elephant. "There were no guardian angels, either in New York or in Washington, to look after her," explained Lesley Barton, her former helmsman. "There was no interest, no support, no enthusiasm for a big liner in the power circles. We believed that she might come back some day, but it was really just wishful thinking. Her era, the age of U.S.-flag liners, had passed." Since 1969, she has been all but abandoned: tormented by the changing weather, given minimal repairs, invaded, and stripped. The badly faded paint on her two enormous funnels alone has not been maintained in over three decades. "It is a very sad sight these days," noted Daniel Trachtenberg in 2001, a former officer with the SS *United States* Preservation Society. "I do not think that there is much hope other than scrapping her or possibly just taking her out to sea and sinking her. By fall, the economic picture for possibly reviving her as a rebuilt cruise ship or making her into a museum or floating hotel seems almost impossible." But rumors continued. In February 2003, it was reported that "firm plans are underway to make the liner into a large casino."

But two months later, on April 14th, in one of the most surprising and long awaited announcements in recent ocean liner history, Miami-based Norwegian Cruise Lines released the news that they were buying not only the *United States*, but another Yankee veteran, the *Independence*. At the time, the 51-year-old *United States* was still lying at Philadelphia and the 52-year-old *Independence* was idle in San Francisco harbor. Both ships are to be rebuilt, with structural work being done in an American shipyard and the final outfitting and decorating in a foreign yard, and are expected to resume American-flag service. While very costly and with uncertain recommissioning dates as we go to press with this book, plans are to use both of these great, historically-important liners on cruises from U.S. ports, including Hawaii and Alaska. Joyously, it seems that the *United States*, after myriad revival rumors and the longest sleep for any liner, will go to sea once again!

With her intended overhaul unexpectedly canceled in November 1969, the *United States* spent several months at the Newport News Shipyard before being moved in June 1970 to an unused cargo berth, the Norfolk International Terminal—her home for almost twenty years (*above*). In that time, rust crept over her hull, the bright paint on her funnels faded, and her interiors grew musty and uninviting. In her seventeen years as an active liner, sailing for United States Lines, she had logged 2.7 million miles and carried just over a million passengers. Now, her wheelhouse telegraph read "finished with engines." Rumors soon started. She was at times reported to become a rebuilt cruise ship, a floating hotel, a missionary center, a conference center, a museum and a roving trade fair with American products. Later, there was news that she would become a casino, moored off Atlantic City, New Jersey. The U.S. Navy probably drew up the most extensive plans for the *United States* as a rebuilt hospital ship with as many as 1,600 beds, based in the Indian Ocean. In a deal worth $4.6 million, she was transferred to the U.S. Maritime Administration in 1973 and, using thirty large dehumidifiers, was made nearly airtight, with all but two entrances on the ship sealed. Yet another plan surfaced to move her to the government's "mothball fleet" in Virginia's James River. Instead, she remained in deepening decline at her Norfolk berth.

The expanding, Oslo-based Norwegian Caribbean Lines, deeply interested in the rapidly expanding Caribbean cruise business out of Florida, considered the *United States* for conversion in 1977–78. Instead, they bought another idle superliner, the *France*, which they rebuilt as their flagship *Norway*, a 67,000-tonner with 2,100 berths that was then the largest cruise ship afloat. Greek shipowners, the Chandris Lines, who had bought the *America* in 1964, were also interested and made some preliminary plans. They wanted to use her on very fast, seventy-day around-the-world itineraries, but later revised the planning for short trips to the Caribbean out of Miami. Ultimately, Chandris Lines' plans for the ship proved unviable, and further talk of purchasing her were abandoned. The *United States*, said to be for sale for as much as $12 million, finally caught the eye of Seattle-based businessman Richard Hadley. He formed United States Cruises, Incorporated, and planned to restyle and thoroughly modernize her as a condominium-style cruise ship, sailing the Atlantic as well as the Pacific. In June 1980, during preparations for the finalization of her sale to Hadley, the *United States* had a brief stay in the big floating dock at Norfolk Shipbuilding & Dry Dock Company (*above*). The dry docking was primarily used for the required inspection of her underwater sections, that once top-secret hull. Note the partially lit twin funnels and the surreal effect created by the twirling tower crane.

The United States Cruises project failed. Only a few investors seemed interested, and the ship, now securely in Hadley's hands, remained the object of rumors. Rebuilding, it was said, would take place variously in Mobile, Hamburg, or even at a Polish shipyard,

and a sailing schedule for 1982 was issued. But again, nothing came to pass. Losing money on the idle ship, Hadley authorized an auction of the ship's fittings in October 1984. Sales were very brisk—a dozen dinner plates sold for up to $4,000, stateroom blankets for $25–50, while the bridge fittings fetched $17,000. For her restaurant in North Carolina's Outer Banks, a collector bought over $300,000 worth of objects: tables, chairs, the 400 lb. ship's bell, and the twenty-foot long, kidney-shaped bar from the first-class ballroom. The builder's plate was later put up for sale at $5,000. Little else happened to the ship itself other than being moved to a CSX coal pier in nearby Newport News. Over time, the ship grew shabbier, like a grand house that had fallen on very hard times. In 1986, Hadley released more elaborate plans: an observation lounge fitted above the bridge, a fifty-seat bar positioned in the forward funnel, and a three-deck shopping mall in place of the aft cargo hatches. But nothing more than increased debts followed. In the winter of 1992, the ship was seized by federal marshals and put up for auction. Turkish "interests," later identified as Marmara Marine, bought her for $2.5 million and, in the summer of 1992, the *United States* was slowly and carefully towed across the Atlantic, to spend several years at anchor off the small port of Tuzla (*opposite, top*). There were frequent reports that she would be refitted at a nearby shipyard and reactivated for further service. Two guards, using a portable stove for light meals, looked after the otherwise empty liner. A launch made a daily trip to the ship, but only under agreeable weather conditions. In 1994, yet more plans were made: the Turks would continue to own her, Sweden's

Effjohn International would manage her, and the Cunard Line would handle the sales and marketing. Once again, she would run seasonal Atlantic crossings, teamed, so it was planned, with the *Queen Elizabeth 2*. Again, a year later, there was a report that she would sail for Greek-owned Regency Cruises, running in the lucrative Caribbean cruise trades as the *Regent States*. Still she waited, ever patiently.

Little was done to the ship other than being stripped of asbestos, lifeboats, and davits during a visit to Sevastopol, the naval port in the Ukraine. While the davits were subsequently cut-up for scrap, some of the lifeboats were sold to Ukrainian fishermen. Most of the interior bulkheads were removed, and two of her propellers, which had been removed, were secured to an aft outer deck. Less and less was left aboard the *United States*. Later, the Turkish owners felt that there was a renewed possibility for U.S.-flag service, especially after a refit in an American shipyard. In July 1996, it was reported that the *United States* had been placed under tow and, at

a cautious speed of 9–10 knots, was making her way back to U.S. shores. Gradually, it was revealed that her destination was the large graving dock at the former Boston Navy Yard. Official permission was subsequently withdrawn, however, and the ship was then said to be headed for New York, berthing either at the Bayonne Military Ocean Terminal in New Jersey or at Brooklyn's near-derelict Bush Terminal docks. Other rumors suggested that she would go to the closed Brooklyn Army Terminal or simply wait at anchor outside the Verrazano Narrows Bridge. In the end, she finally docked in Philadelphia at a container cargo pier quite close to the Walt Whitman Bridge, where she is seen in this view dated July 27, 1996 (*above*). It was later said that she would be converted for cruising in the closed Philadelphia Naval Shipyard, which was to be revived by private developers. Soon afterward, no less than five port cities—Charleston, Savannah, Jacksonville, New Orleans, and San Francisco—were said to be interested in obtaining the ship as a combination hotel-conference center.

In the fall of 1997, the *United States* was moved to Pier 82, another unused cargo berth in Philadelphia, where she is seen here on November 22, 1997 (***above***). At the time of this writing (2002), this is her current home. At the same time, she was again seized by U.S. marshals, since the Turks still owed as much as $2 million on their $2.5 million purchase price from 1992. New Jersey–based businessman Edward Cantor bought her at auction for $6 million, again with plans for revival as a cruise liner. Mystery concerning her future, of course, continued to surround her. Cantor soon changed his mind, offering the ship for sale at a vastly inflated $33–35 million. Expectedly, there were no takers. Alternatively, her scrap value was estimated to be $2 million.

The great enclosed Promenade Deck (***opposite, top***), where John Wayne, the Eisenhowers, Rita Hayworth and the Duke and Duchess of Windsor once strolled, is now silent and desolate.

The First-Class Dining Room is a shell of its former self, having been stripped down to the structural fittings (***opposite, middle***).

The wheelhouse, from which the Blue Riband was captured, is also empty and barren (***opposite, bottom***).

The great funnels were badly faded by the late 1990s (*opposite, top*). They were, however, lit once again during the Fourth of July weekend in 1999. Robert Wogan, an artist with a specialty in "obsolete machinery," was given permission by the owners and, using several generators and 70 lb. floodlights, illuminated the stacks for brief periods on the three evenings. There were other plans for the funnels as well. Officials and planners in Brooklyn, New York wanted to develop long stretches of their neglected waterfront. One plan was to berth the *United States* at Pier 1, at the foot of Fulton Street and just across from Lower Manhattan. An alternative site was the old Brooklyn Navy Yard. "The Brooklyn Navy Yard project would have required removing those two, mammoth funnels, which in itself would have cost as much as $300,000, to clear the Brooklyn and the Manhattan Bridges along the East River," noted Daniel Trachtenberg, a former officer of the *SS United States* Foundation, a special interest group that wants to see the ship saved at all costs. "The stacks would have been placed on a barge, floated in separately and then reattached. The federal government wanted to see the Navy Yard area developed and even sent a team out to southern California to study the *Queen Mary*."

Rainwater has been accumulating along the lower decks in recent years, and the last remains of the fuel oil placed aboard in 1969 has also been leaking. The ship has been described in recent times as being "quiet, very dark, and totally stripped." Some locals became interested in the ship and a few even jumped fences to get a closer view of the knifelike bow. Here we see the foredeck just above (*opposite, bottom*). The ship's deteriorated condition made

some onlookers think that she had been sunk and then salvaged. They compared her to the *Titanic*.

By 2000, new plans for the ship (*above*) included having it remade as a medical treatment and research center while berthed at New York's Pier 84, adjacent to the USS *Intrepid* Sea-Air-Space Museum. Another firm has drawn up plans using the liner as a hotel, a project dubbed the "Flotel *United States*," also docked at Manhattan's redeveloped West Side, either at Pier 76 or Pier 94. Again, nothing was finalized. Her owner, Edward Cantor, died in February 2002 and her future became even more uncertain. "I would be thrilled to see the *United States* restored as a stationary monument to our brilliant shipbuilding and shipping heritage," said ocean-liner historian and preservationist Peter Knego. "Naturally, I would prefer New York, but I would be very happy to see her anywhere just as long as those two funnels get a fresh coat of paint and her profile remains relatively untouched." While it seemed unlikely for so long, the wishes of Peter Knego and legions of others seem to be coming true. On April 14, 2003, Norwegian Cruise Lines, itself owned by Malaysia's giant Star Cruises, announced their plans to buy the *United States* and the idle *Independence*, and rebuild, modernize, and restore them to American-flag passenger ship service. The *United States* will have new and happier chapters in her later history—she will sail again! In the meantime, this book is a small tribute, a photographic reminder, and a salute on the fiftieth anniversary of her maiden voyage: July 3, 1952–2002. Three blasts to the SS *United States*—indeed, the greatest ocean liner of her time!

Bibliography

Braynard, Frank O. *By Their Works Ye Shall Know Them*. New York: Gibbs & Cox, 1968.

——. *Lives of the Liners*. New York: Cornell Maritime Press, 1947.

Braynard, Frank O. & Miller, William H. *Fifty Famous Liners*, Vols 1–5. Cambridge, England: Patrick Stephens, Ltd, 1982–86.

Duffy, Francis J. & Miller, William H. *The New York Harbor Book*. Falmouth, Maine: TBW Books, 1986.

Dunn, Laurence. *Passenger Liners*. Southampton, England: Adlard Coles, Ltd, 1961, 1965 (rev. ed.).

Emmons, Frederick E. *American Passenger Ships 1873–1983*. Newark, Delaware: University of Delaware Press, 1985.

Farrington, S. Kip. *Ships of the U.S. Merchant Marine*. New York: E. P. Dutton & Co., Inc., 1947.

Kludas, Arnold. *Great Passenger Ships of the World, Vols 1–5*. Cambridge, England: Patrick Stephens, Ltd, 1972–76.

Le Fleming, H. M. *Ocean Ships*. London: Ian Allan, Ltd., 1961.

Miller, William H. *Passenger Liners American Style*. London: Carmania Press, Ltd, 1999.

——. *Picture History of American Passenger Ships*. Mineola, New York: Dover Publications, Inc., 2001.

——. SS *United States: The History of America's Greatest Liner*. Sparkford, England: Patrick Stephens, Ltd, 1991.

——. *The Last Atlantic Liners*. London: Conway Maritime Press, Ltd, 1985.

Moody, Bert. *Ocean Ships*. London: Ian Allan, Ltd., 1971.

——. *Ocean Ships*. London: Ian Allan, Ltd., 1978.

Official Steamship Guide. New York: Transportation Guides, Inc, 1937–63.

Sawyer, L. A. & Mitchell, W. H. *From America to United States* (four volumes). Kendal, Westmorland, England: World Ship Society, 1979–86.

——. *Victory Ships & Tankers*. Cambridge, Maryland: Cornell Maritime Press, Inc., 1974.

Ships & Sailing. Milwaukee, Wisconsin: Kalmbach Publishing Co., 1950–60.

Squarey, C. M. *The Patient Talks*. London: Thomas Cook & Son, Ltd, 1955.

Towline. New York: Moran Towing & Transportation Co., 1950–98.

Index of Ships

Many of the ships mentioned in this book have carried different names during their careers.
With a few exceptions, only the name most relevant to the text is reflected in this index.